Choose your FOOD to change your MOOD

Με
σου χαρίζω αυτό το βιβλίο
όχι μόνο να θυμάσαι εμένα
αλλά για αυτό το κομμάτι
της ζωής σου που πέρα-
σες εδώ στην Οξφόρδη
γεμάτο χαρές, λύπες,
θλίψεις, αγωνίες, ευτυχίες,
απογοητεύσεις, παρηγοριές,
ή κ διασκεδάσεις.
Πως προσπαθούσαμε να
φτιάξουμε το mood μας!!

Πόλυ

Choose your FOOD to change your MOOD

Steven Saunders

Simon G. Brown

CARROLL & BROWN PUBLISHERS LIMITED

Text © Simon Brown and Steven Saunders 1999
Recipes © Steven Saunders 1999
Illustrations and compilation © Carroll & Brown Limited 1999

Previously published in 1999 in the United Kingdom as Feng Shui Food by Thorsons

Project Editor Jennifer Mussett
Managing Art Editor Adelle Morris
Designers Sandra Brooke, Gilda Pacitti
Illustrator Sandra Brooke
Photography David Murray, Jules Selmes

A CIP catalogue record for this book is available from the British Library.

ISBN 1-903258-64-2

10987654321

Reproduced by Colourscan, Singapore
Printed and bound in Singapore by Tien Wah Press

contents

This book shows you how to create dishes that not only taste sensational but can also bring about positive changes in your life. By applying the art of Feng Shui to preparing, cooking and serving food, you can improve your health, boost your energy, strengthen your relationships and promote household harmony – not to mention get more from your meals. The first chapter sets out the principles of Feng Shui and explains how different ingredients and cooking methods, together with the layout and decor of the kitchen and dining area, can affect your feelings and well-being. Once you have acquired this basic understanding, you can plan the perfect menu and adjust your dining area to ensure health and happiness.

the principles

1

feng shui and chi energy

ACCORDING TO EASTERN TRADITION, chi is a powerful universal energy that flows through the sun and its planets, the air, all objects, all plants and animals, and every human being. Although we cannot see or feel it like the other forces of nature, we can become emotionally aware of it, as though through a sixth sense.

The ancient art of Feng Shui is based on the theory that everything is imbued with chi, and that it forms, exists within and empowers all aspects of life. As chi energy passes through an object, it takes on the character of the chi of that object – as thoughts, ideas and emotions – and vice versa. Thus, chi energy both influences and is influenced by everything it touches, and therefore is continuously in a state of flux.

Everything in your environment affects you and your chi, including the weather, the landscape, the building you live in, the space you work in, the people you spend time with, and the food you eat. The goal of Feng Shui is to keep your chi healthy and boost the forces that you need in your life. If, for example, you need to relax, you can use Feng Shui to slow down your chi energy. If your surroundings and the food you eat contain calming chi, these can influence your personal chi force too.

THE CHI IN FOOD

Every type of food has a chi energy of its own, determined by its shape, colour, texture, and even the climate, soil and manner in which it grew. A root vegetable that drives its way through hard soil, such as a carrot, has a more forceful chi energy than one that grows out of the soil, such a marrow or pumpkin. The same principles apply to fish and meat. Active fish, such as salmon and trout, have a more dynamic chi energy, while fish or seafoods of a gentle nature have a more gentle chi energy. Eat squid, oysters and mussels if you wish to relax more. A similar theory applies to meat, and it is worth looking at the character of the animal. A chicken has a more nervous, restless chi energy while a cow has a more docile nature. In theory, you will take in the character of any food you eat on a regular basis.

The foods that contain the greatest amount of chi energy are those that can be called 'living foods'. These include vegetables, fruit, wholegrains, beans and seeds, all of which begin or continue to grow after they have been harvested, given the right conditions. Highly processed foods, on the other hand, absorb chi energy from the factory or plant in which they are produced. This

A WILD SALMON THAT SWIMS UPSTREAM AND JUMPS WATERFALLS HAS A POWERFUL CHI ENERGY. IF YOU WANT TO BE MORE DYNAMIC, EAT WILD SALMON.

gives them a less natural chi energy. Certain foods, such as meat and fish, carry some of the negative energy of being caught and killed. Along with processed foods, they are essentially 'dead foods'. As a result, it would be advantageous to avoid eating meat if you don't want to take in the negative chi from animals that have been reared and killed. For similar reasons, dairy products also are not recommended except in small quantities.

The more natural the farming practice, the better the chi. Organic farms aim to produce food without synthetic pesticides, fertilisers, battery conditions and added hormones, thus removing the health risks involved in consuming unnaturally produced foods. By choosing organic food, you are improving your health and promoting positive chi in the world around you. If you do eat meat or dairy foods, try to buy organic products. The recipes throughout *Choose your Food to Change your Mood* are for vegetarian or seafood dishes, except for four meat recipes in Chapter 2. Dairy foods and eggs are not considered healthy and are therefore not featured heavily. Non-dairy options are indicated where appropriate.

The origin of your food is vital to the chi it provides. If the food is grown locally, it stays fresh for longer, and it won't have picked up so much negative chi energy from lengthy or unhealthy transportation. If food is produced in a foreign climate, it will provide a different kind of chi that is not always appropriate. An orange from Africa, for example, provides fresh and cooling chi to counter the warm climate. It may not be right for northern Europeans, for whom a warming local root vegetable is preferable.

THE CHI ALL AROUND YOU

Every building has its own chi energy that influences the chi energy of the people, objects and activities within that space. As chi energy flows through a building, it changes according to the shapes, colours and materials of the surfaces inside. The positions of the rooms and doors determine how chi energy flows into, out of and through a building. Long corridors, rows of doors, and stairs leading down to an entrance all cause chi energy to move too quickly, making a space less relaxing. An absence of natural light, clutter and a surfeit of upholstered surfaces, on the other hand, can cause chi energy to move slowly and stagnate.

The chi energy in your home will influence the chi in your kitchen and dining room, affecting the food that you prepare and the atmosphere in which you eat. Use the advice on pages 22–25 to optimise the chi energy in your kitchen. For information on how to keep your chi energy positive for encouraging a conducive atmosphere for romance or family harmony, for example, see chapter 3. Finally, you can use the advice in Chapter 5 for choosing the right restaurant for your mood.

feng shui and
yin and yang

THERE ARE TWO TYPES OF CHI ENERGY within every entity, including ourselves – yin and yang. Yin is the passive energy, promoting reflection, relaxation and creativity. Yang is the active energy, stimulating movement, progress and activity. Yin and yang are mutually interdependent; they feed each other and are equally important to the individual. Everyone at any one time is made up of differing degrees of yin and yang, and this relationship will affect a person's character and behaviour. However, the proportion of yin and yang will change through time according to the external chi influences.

According to Eastern tradition, yin and yang energies should be as equal as possible. The aim of Feng Shui is to balance the energies through controlling your surroundings and greater environment, including the food that you eat.

THE PRINCIPLES

According to Eastern tradition, yin and yang energies exist according to a number of rules, summarised here into three main principles. Firstly, everything is either more yin or more yang in relation to other things. For example, a potato is more yin than a salmon, yet less yin than an apple. And nothing is wholly yin or wholly yang – everything has some yin and some yang energy, even if it is a very small portion. It may help to consider entities as varying shades of grey, rather than either black or white.

Secondly, everything seeks a state of balance. If you are more yin, for example, you will naturally try to counter this with yang influences, even though you may do this at a subconcious level. In this way, yin and yang are said to attract each other.

Lastly, the yin and yang in everything is constantly changing. The relationship between all things is such that you are always in the process of being influenced and changed by your environment.

YIN AND YANG TENDENCIES

Everyone has both yin and yang elements, although most of us probably find that we are more yin or more yang. This imbalance may be just a temporary state, such as a lethargic period occurring as a result of too much yin, or it may be a more general ongoing problem. Use the chart opposite to work out whether you have an imbalance and in which direction it lies. Judge whether it is a temporary stance or a part of yourself that has been present for many years; long-term or very strong imbalances may take longer to remedy.

THE YIN AND YANG SYMBOL REPRESENTS THE RELATIONSHIP BETWEEN THE TWO FORCES — THE TWO SHAPES FIT TOGETHER TO FORM A COMPLETE CIRCLE. THE EYE OF EACH SHAPE IS THE OPPOSITE COLOUR, SYMBOLISING THE SEED OF THE OPPOSITE ENERGY GROWING WITHIN EACH FORCE.

CREATE THE BEST COMBINATION OF YIN AND YANG IN YOUR LIFE TO CHARGE YOUR CHI ENERGIES IN A POSITIVE DIRECTION.

Your mood and the way you react to events depend on whether you feel more yin or yang at a particular time. Too much of one can result in inappropriate or unnecessarily strong emotions. If, for example, you wake up feeling depressed for no reason, your reaction may be a result of too much yin energy. If, on the other hand, you lose your temper over something small, it may be caused by overpowering yang energy. Keeping your energies aligned can help you feel more emotionally balanced and better able to cope with difficult situations.

When you are healthily yang, you are likely to feel confident, assertive, enthusiastic, in control and that you can go out and make things happen. If, however, you become too yang, you can become aggressive, impatient, intolerant, domineering and frustrated. Over a long period of time, being too yang can lead to physical problems, such as stiff, tense muscles; digestive problems; headaches in the back of your head; constipation; sleeping difficulties and an increased risk of arterial disease. You can address these problems by adding yin energies to your diet and surroundings.

are you too yin or too yang?

LOOK DOWN THE LISTS BELOW and choose one or two words that best describe you and your lifestyle. Are they nearer the yang end at the top or nearer the yin end at the bottom? Compare yourself to other people; if you are an enthusiastic leader, for example, you are probably more yang. Most people will find that they are slightly yin in some aspects and yang in others – a healthy balance. However, if your character is strongly yin or yang, you may find that you are experiencing unnecessary difficulties. You should attempt to redress the situation by altering your diet and surroundings, using the advice given in this book.

POSITIVE EMOTIONS	NEGATIVE EMOTIONS	MENTAL QUALITIES	SKILLS AND INTERESTS
ambitious	angry	quick thinking	problem solving
enthusiastic	frustrated	detailed	accounting
confident	competitive	precise	practical cooking
reassured	irritable	logical	creative cooking
relaxed	anxious	ordered	socialising
peaceful	tearful	creative	writing
gentle	insecure	broad-minded	painting
sensitive	depressed	imaginative	philosophising

YIN and YANG in your diet

EAT YIN FOODS TO reduce stress, improve your social skills, be more spiritual, release your creative spirit, relax and unwind properly, become more understanding and sympathetic, broaden your mind and your imagination, take the time to understand problems before tackling them, see things from a wider perspective, and find compassion for others.

YIN
- PASSIVE
- DARK
- COLD
- MIDNIGHT
- WINTER
- WATER

EAT YANG FOODS TO feel more self-confident and assertive, improve your efficiency and thinking, boost your energy in the winter, find fast, practical solutions to problems, build enthusiasm and motivation for a job or task, increase your ambition and competitive drive, focus your mental and physical skills, work quickly through problems, and learn to stand up for yourself.

YANG
- ACTIVE
- LIGHT
- HEAT
- MIDDAY
- SUMMER
- FIRE

If you are healthily yin, you may feel a sense of inner peace and be relaxed, content with life, receptive to new ideas and concepts, comfortable with other people, in harmony with nature and able to go with the flow. Too much yin energy, however, may leave you feeling depressed, pessimistic, disheartened, unable to feel motivated, hopeless, tearful and sad. You may also feel unable to do anything, a lack courage and motivation, and you may even come to believe that life isn't worth living. Going through a long period of being too yin can also result in physical symptoms, such as feeling cold; being more susceptible to infectious illnesses; experiencing poor circulation, fluid retention, low energy levels, difficulty in getting up in the morning, lethargy, headaches at the front of your head and diarrhoea. To remedy these problems, you need to realign your chi energy by adding yang energies to your diet and surroundings.

ACHIEVING THE RIGHT BALANCE WITH FOOD

One of the most powerful tools of Feng Shui and Eastern medicine is the ability to balance yin and yang energies to promote complete health and optimum performance. The primary aim is to locate an imbalance in your behaviour, physical health or emotions. You can then use food and your surroundings to redress the problem by aligning your yin and yang chi energy.

Each food is more yin or more yang than other foods. By choosing the right sorts of food, you can feed your yin or yang energy. The information opposite explains which foods are yin and which are yang. Using this a guide, you can prescribe your own remedy to counter a yin/yang imbalance. If, for example, you are lacking assertion, you need more yang energy in the form of a seafood dish. You can also help boost your yang energies by avoiding foods that have strong yin energies, such as soft drinks or sweet foods and sugar.

In addition to its type, other characteristics also alter a food's chi energy and yin/yang balance, notably the colour, shape and the way that it is prepared and cooked.

Food preparation influences chi energy, mainly because it changes the moisture, texture, shape and even the colour and taste of the food. If you change the shape by chopping it into small bits you add more yin energy, and if you then liquidize it, you make it very yin. The colour of food also has an impact on the type of chi energy it will have. The lists on the top of page 14 detail how colours affect food, from yang at the top to yin at the bottom: yellow is a more balanced colour.

Consider how you cook your food, using the information on page 14 to guide you. In general, the longer that you cook food, the more yang it becomes.

Your food can also be made more yin or yang with seasonings and flavourings. Add rice syrup to stewed apple and you make it yin; add salt and it is more yang. Wine can also be used to make a dish more yin, while shoyu sauce makes food more yang.

yang

sea salt

meat

eggs

chicken

fish

seafood

hard cheeses

bread

rice

pasta

beans

root vegetables

soft cheeses

butter

milk

yoghurt

leafy green
vegetables

tofu

nuts and seeds

fruit

sugar

liquids

yin

THE LIST SHOWS THE GRADATION
OF FOODS FROM THE MOST YANG,
AT THE TOP, TO THE MOST YIN,
AT THE BOTTOM.

yin and yang types of food

A FOOD IS CONSIDERED YIN OR YANG mainly according to its type – a salmon, for example, is yang, while an apple is yin. As a general rule, yang foods generate heat and often contain plenty of protein and fat. Meat, fish and eggs are good examples. Yin foods, on the other hand, are generally cooling and contain more liquid and sweetness; blackcurrants, yoghurt and orange juice are more yin.

Generally, you should aim to blend ingredients to make a balanced meal that combines yin and yang favourably. However, if you want to use food to rebalance your energies, choose a meal that is more yin or yang. Improve your yin energy, for example, with a yin dish, such as a vegetable soup (see page 32). A more yang dish, such as poached salmon (see page 43), would be needed if you want to boost your yang energies.

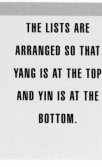

COOKING METHODS

Baking

Pressure cooking

Stewing and casseroling

Simmering

Deep-frying

Sautéing

Stir-frying

Steaming

Blanching

Raw

FLAVOURINGS

Sea salt

Shoyu sauce

Ginger

Garlic

Natural vinegars – cider
  or rice vinegar

Fruit juices

Barley malt or rice syrup

Wine, beer or sake

Sugar or honey

COLOURS

Red

Orange

Yellow

Pale green

Pale blue

MATERIALS

Hard stone

Glazed tiles

Porous tiles

Metal

Hard woods

Soft woods

Soft fabrics

The recipes in Chapter 2 have been developed to enable you to cook your own yin and yang dishes. The type of food, preparation techniques, flavourings and cooking style have all been carefully considered during the development of each recipe. You have a choice between two similar main ingredients, such as crab and tuna. One dish is more yin and one is more yang. The more yin dish, such as the delicately prepared tian of crab, is featured on the left-hand page, and the more yang dish – pan-fried tuna cakes – is on the right-hand page (see pages 38–39). It must be noted that these dishes are only yin and yang compared with each other.

AN AIRY ROOM CAN BE DESIGNED USING LIGHT AND COOLING YIN ELEMENTS IN THE FURNISHINGS TO MAKE IT RELAXING.

YOUR SURROUNDINGS

The yin and yang energies in the environment where you prepare and eat food can greatly influence your personal energies. Feng Shui aims to optimise your chi energy by showing you how to arrange your furniture, colour schemes and decorative objects around you in order to balance the yin and yang energies in your home. Keep a good blend of yin and yang unless you need to influence your life with one or the other.

COLOURS Colours have a powerful impact on your outer chi energy field and therefore tend also to have an immediate effect on your emotions. Colours apply to the overall decoration of a room as well

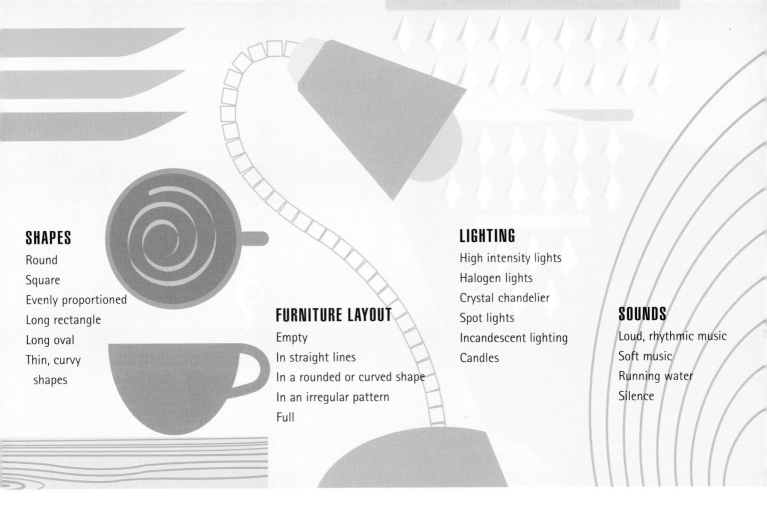

SHAPES

Round
Square
Evenly proportioned
Long rectangle
Long oval
Thin, curvy
    shapes

FURNITURE LAYOUT

Empty
In straight lines
In a rounded or curved shape
In an irregular pattern
Full

LIGHTING

High intensity lights
Halogen lights
Crystal chandelier
Spot lights
Incandescent lighting
Candles

SOUNDS

Loud, rhythmic music
Soft music
Running water
Silence

as the items within the room, such as pictures, flowers or pieces of art. The colours of the food you eat, the crockery you use and any accompanying table linen or centrepiece are also important.

SHAPES The shapes of items in your home impact on and influence the way the energy flows around a room. This applies to large items of furniture, such as tables and chairs, as well as smaller objects, such as glassware and dishes.

MATERIALS Certain surfaces are more yang and speed up the flow of chi energy – marble or tile floors or counter tops, for example. Other surfaces are more yin and will calm the energy – such as wooden floors, upholstered chairs and

CREATE A MORE DYNAMIC ATMOSPHERE
BY FURNISHING AND DECORATING
WITH YANG ELEMENTS.

tablecloths. As a general guideline, if a surface is shiny and impermeable, it will produce a yang atmosphere. Non-shiny, permeable materials create yin energy.

LAYOUT The more open, empty and regimented the layout, the more quickly the chi energy flows and the more yang it will feel. A room that is filled with furniture is more yin, especially if it is not placed in an orderly arrangement.

LIGHTING The softer and lower the lighting, the more yin the atmosphere, whereas brighter direct lighting creates a more active yang atmosphere.

SOUNDS Loud or rhythmic music enlivens the yang energy in a room, while soft music with no rhythm is yin.

the principles of
the five elements

ACCORDING TO CLASSICAL EASTERN PRINCIPLES, there are five elemental forces – tree, fire, soil, metal and water – each of which has a number of distinct characteristics. The elemental force of fire, for example, is full of passion and excitement, while the element of soil has a secure and comforting energy. Each element also has a season and is represented by colours, shapes and materials; for example, water is the quiet, black, winter element. The energies are all around us, within us and exist throughout the universe, influencing our health and emotions – both positively and negatively. Ideally, the five elements should exist in balance, although frequently one may dominate, bringing about a continually shifting energy pattern. When one element is dominant, it results in an imbalance that can influence the way that you think and feel. Feng Shui aims to balance the five elements so that they all work together in harmony. The art of locating and realigning a five element imbalance is one of the more technical and intricate skills used in Feng Shui.

THE RELATIONSHIPS BETWEEN THE ELEMENTS

The five elements interact via a network of supportive and destructive links. Each element supports one other element and destroys another. In turn, that element is supported by an element and destroyed by another. This is known as the cycles of support and destruction, depicted in the diagram opposite.

The elements are arranged in a circle in the following order; fire, soil, metal, water and tree. In the supportive cycle, each element nourishes its next-door neighbour in a clockwise direction. For example, fire energy supports soil, and so on. As long as each element is balanced, this arrangement should create a reasonable state of harmony. However, if the element being supported becomes too strong, it has the effect of draining its supporting element. So, if soil becomes too strong, it will drain fire.

When one element is strong and the element next in the clockwise direction is comparatively weak, the chi energy will shift into the pattern of the destructive cycle. In this situation,

PROMOTES life, growth, vitality, activity

SEASON spring

POSITIVE EMOTIONS confidence, assertiveness, endurance

NEGATIVE EMOTIONS anger, irritability, hyperactivity

COLOURS green or blue

SHAPES tall and rectangular

MATERIALS wood, bamboo, paper

PROMOTES passion, warmth, excitement, expression

SEASON early/mid summer

POSITIVE EMOTIONS excitement, passion, exuberance

NEGATIVE EMOTIONS hysteria, stress, emotional disturbance

COLOURS bright red or purple

SHAPES triangular, serrated, spikes

MATERIALS lights, candles, naked flame

PROMOTES comfort, security, steadiness, caution

SEASON late summer/early autumn

POSITIVE EMOTIONS sympathy, consideration, understanding

NEGATIVE EMOTIONS jealousy, dependence, indecision

COLOURS yellow, beige and brown

SHAPES low, flat and rectangular

MATERIALS clay, ceramic, cotton, wool, soft stone, bricks

the strong element will not support the next, weaker element, but will skip over it and destroy the following element. So, if fire becomes dominant and soil is weak, then soil will not be supported and metal will receive the destructive force of the fire. Each element is therefore destructive to one element and can be destroyed by another.

When an element becomes dominant, there is a tendency for it to remain so to the detriment of the other elements and to the chi energy of the environment. If, for example, fire is powerful, it will become progressively more dominant, destroying metal, draining tree and throwing the balance into disarray. Feng

IN THE SUPPORTIVE CYCLE, EACH ELEMENT SUPPORTS THE NEXT IN A CLOCKWISE DIRECTION. IF THE NEXT ELEMENT IS WEAK, THE ELEMENTS WILL SHIFT INTO THE DESTRUCTIVE CYCLE, AND AN ELEMENT WILL DESTROY THE SECOND ELEMENT IN A CLOCKWISE DIRECTION.

Shui can be used to redress imbalances; below, you will discover ways to support weaker elements and deflect or weaken the energy of dominant elements.

THE FIVE ELEMENTS AND YOU

Every person's individual chi energy contains each one of the five elements to a lesser or greater degree. However, there is rarely symmetry in the five elements, and one element is frequently more dominant, causing the element pattern to continually shift. For a period of time you may, for example, be influenced predominantly by the element of fire, before it suddenly burns itself out, after which water may become dominant.

You can use the five elements to boost your energies in a certain direction. If, for example, you want to become more assertive, you should increase the tree element in your life. You can achieve this through eating more leafy green vegetables and by placing plenty of wooden objects and plants around your home. You can make this tree energy even more powerful by including more water energy in your life at the same time, because water is tree's supporting element. Make your leafy green vegetables into a soup or stew with plenty of water and place

PROMOTES richness, solidity, leadership, organisation

SEASON late autumn

POSITIVE EMOTIONS orderliness, self-reflection, sexual fervour

NEGATIVE EMOTIONS depression, sadness, introversion

COLOURS white, grey, rusty red, silver or gold

SHAPES round, arches and oval

MATERIALS metals, hard stone

PROMOTES depth, power, flexibility, tranquillity

SEASON winter

POSITIVE EMOTIONS courage, inspiration, flexibility

NEGATIVE EMOTIONS fear, lack of self-esteem, worry

COLOURS black or cream

SHAPES irregular, wavy and curved

MATERIALS glass

five element foods

IF YOU NEED TO ENHANCE a particular element, you should add more of the relevant taste into your diet. If you want to increase your confidence and assertiveness, for example, you need to boost your tree energy by eating plenty of sour foods, such as pickles. To prevent this energy from being drained by the fire element, reduce bitter fire-type tastes in ingredients. You also should prevent tree energy from being destroyed by the metal element, so don't eat pungent foods, such as garlic and ginger, without taking plenty of water ingredients.

To obtain a perfect balance, you also should try to include aspects of each of the five elements in the way your meal is prepared and cooked. If you want to improve a particular element, use the cooking method of that element and its supporting element; avoid the cooking method of the destructive element.

TREE
SOUR
olives, vinegar, sauerkraut, pickles

COOKING METHOD
steaming, blanching

FIRE
BITTER
spring onions, bitter lemon, watercress, roasted seeds, chilli

COOKING METHOD
stir-frying, pan-roasting, tempura

SOIL
SWEET
corn, peas, syrups, cooked fruits, sweet vegetables

COOKING METHOD
poaching, stewing, long cooking in a little water

METAL
PUNGENT
ginger, garlic, mustard, radish, brown rice

COOKING METHOD
baking, pressure cooking

WATER
SALTY
miso, shoyu sauce, winter greens, kelp, salty fish

COOKING METHOD
boiling, simmering, soups

water features in the part of your home that gets the morning sun – the direction for growth and activity (see the Eight directions, pages 20–21).

As is the case with yin and yang, an imbalance in the five elements can eventually result in a loss of energy, ill health, and inappropriate feelings, reactions and behaviour. If you have too much fire, for example, you will feel impassioned and excitable. You may, however, also become hysterical, and find yourself reacting to situations with strong outbursts that drain your energy and make your life stressful and difficult, resulting in further problems.

Check the list of positive and negative emotions associated with each symbol on pages 16–17 to determine if you are more influenced by one element over the others. If so, you will need to reduce the impact of this element in your life. Using the cycles to drain chi energy from the previous element, you also can change your environment to moderate the strong and support the weak. If, for example, you want to calm your fire energy, as well as avoiding fire influences, you should the following weak soil element to drain fire energy or, in extreme cases, activate water energy to destroy fire energy. Soil will help you to calm down naturally and regain a balanced approach to your life.

THIS ROOM BLENDS ALL THE ELEMENTS, WITH FIRE ENERGY IN THE NATURAL AND OVERHEAD LIGHT, WATER ENERGY IN THE GLASS WINDOWS AND VASE, TREE ENERGY IN THE WOODEN FLOOR, METAL IN THE TABLE, AND SOIL ENERGY IN THE FABRIC OF THE CHAIRS.

MANIPULATING THE ELEMENTS AT HOME

When decorating a dining room or any space in which you habitually eat, try to maintain a balance of the five elements in the materials, colours and features of the room. Use the information on each symbol on pages 16–17 as a guide. If your room has a wooden floor, plaster walls and ceiling, and large windows, it has the elements of tree, soil and water respectively. Bright sunshine will add fire energy, otherwise use bright lights, candles or a real fire. However, such a room may be deficient in metal energy and your meals may become disorganised or less structured. Therefore, it would be advantageous for you to add metal energy in the form of a metallic work of art, clock or other articles, such as cutlery, and by using the colours white and grey.

Specific decorative items are frequently used in Feng Shui to redress five-element imbalances, and should be placed in the appropriate position within the room (see the Eight directions, pages 20–21). Tree features include plants, wood, bamboo and wicker. Fire is added with lights and candles. Provide more soil energy with clay or ceramic objects or a small dish of charcoal. Metal clocks, windchimes or ornaments can boost metal energy. You can add water energy by placing crystals or water features, such as an aquarium, in your home.

how to use
the eight directions

ACCORDING TO FENG SHUI, the character of the chi energy depends on the direction of the compass that it is facing, travelling towards or within. The flow of chi energy from the south, for example, encompasses a passionate, fiery energy that affects every person and object it encounters. Each direction is also linked with one of the five elements and a time of day. Learning to use these energies to their greatest advantage is one of the cornerstones of the art of Feng Shui.

The direction that a building faces and the position of its entrance and rooms influence the make-up of its chi energy. If a kitchen lies in the east of a house, for example, it is influenced by lively eastern chi, good for new projects and enthusiasm and thus for attempting new recipes and styles of cooking with fresh ideas and plenty of energy. However, a dining room here might not benefit from eastern energy as diners could be overactive and unable to relax. The same theory applies to the directions within a room and around a dining table; if you are seated facing east, you may find it hard to sit still.

Feng Shui aims to make the most of good chi and counter the problems created by inappropriate chi. One way it does so is through the use of the five elements. You can place appropriately constructed items around a room to alter the dominant element and adjust the atmosphere to better suit the room's activities. A dining room in the south, which is dominated by bright fire energy, can be made more relaxing with balancing soil and metal elements, such as clay, ceramic and metal objects. You should avoid bright lights too, as these further enhance the fire energy. The five element colours can be used in the same way to strengthen weak elements and calm dominating elements.

Chapter 3 focuses on a number of meal occasions, each one requiring a different chi energy to encourage the best atmosphere. Each occasion in Chapter 3 requires that you and your guests sit facing a particular direction to put you in the right mood for the occasion. To find out which of the eight directions influences your dining room, follow the instructions opposite. Once you have the direction of your dining room, work out the

EAST
TIME OF DAY sunrise
CHARACTER fresh and positive
HELPFUL FOR vitality, new projects and motivation
ELEMENT tree

SOUTH-EAST
TIME OF DAY late morning
CHARACTER busy and active
HELPFUL FOR growth, harmony and creativity
ELEMENT tree

SOUTH
TIME OF DAY midday
CHARACTER bright, fiery, proud and colourful
HELPFUL FOR being noticed, expressive and social
ELEMENT fire

SOUTH-WEST
TIME OF DAY afternoon
CHARACTER supportive, nourishing and cautious
HELPFUL FOR consolidation and methodical progress
ELEMENT soil

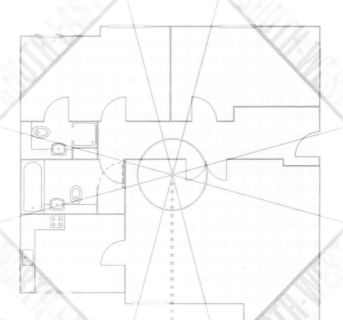

directions around your dining table. Place a compass in the centre of your table and adjust it so that it points north. Work out the rest of the directions from this, remembering that it is the direction that a person is facing that will affect behaviour. Make use of the relationships between the five elements (see page 16–19) and the more detailed advice found in Chapter 3 to create a specific atmosphere.

FIND THE DIRECTIONS OF YOUR HOME

First, make a scale plan of your home, floor by floor. Do this by measuring the walls, doors and windows and any pieces of large furniture. Divide each measurement by the same number so that the scale is small enough to draw onto a sheet of graph paper. Glue your plan onto a piece of cardboard and cut it out.

Find the central point by placing the cutout on the point of a skewer or a sharp pencil and moving it until it balances on the point. Mark this centre point with a pen.

To locate north on your floor plan, first ensure that your plan is facing exactly the same direction as your home by placing the front door of your plan along the inside of your front door. Then use a compass to find the line north from the centre and draw it onto your plan.

Trace the grid above, place it over your plan and match the centres and lines pointing north. Mark onto your plan the boundaries of each of the eight directions and write the initials of each direction inside each segment. You can also put the grid over the centre of each room, or in the centre of your dining table, to find the eight directions of these.

WEST	NORTH-WEST	NORTH	NORTH-EAST
TIME OF DAY sunset	TIME OF DAY dusk	TIME OF DAY night	TIME OF DAY early morning haze
CHARACTER relaxed, reflective and content	CHARACTER wise, responsible and dignified	CHARACTER quiet, restful and still	CHARACTER sharp, active and competitive
HELPFUL FOR romance, pleasure and enjoyment	HELPFUL FOR leadership, planning and organising	HELPFUL FOR regeneration, healing and spirituality	HELPFUL FOR motivation and hard work
ELEMENT metal	ELEMENT metal	ELEMENT water	ELEMENT soil

feng shui and
the kitchen

MAINTAINING A BALANCE OF CHI ENERGY in the cooking area is crucial to family well-being and harmony since a poor energy flow in the kitchen can lead to less healthy chi energy throughout the home. The position of the kitchen within the building, therefore, is particularly important in determining the type of ambient chi energy. To identify the direction in which your kitchen lies, use the method described on page 21. Ideally, your kitchen should be in one of the directions associated with tree energy, as this is harmonious with both the fire energy of the cooker and the water energy of the sink. Without the tree energy completing the five element cycle, the energy between water and fire in your kitchen may become unhealthy. The implications of each of the eight directions for your kitchen – with the most favourable first – are set out below, as well as guidelines on how you can improve the flow of chi in your kitchen if it faces one of the less auspicious directions.

EAST AND SOUTH-EAST These two directions are ideal for positioning your kitchen as the chi energy here is supportive to growth, activity and development. The five element energy in these directions is tree energy, which creates a harmonious flow of chi energy through the kitchen and benefits the whole home.

THE KITCHEN IS CONSIDERED THE PLACE THAT CREATES LIFE FOR THE FAMILY BECAUSE IT IS THE ROOM IN WHICH THE FOOD IS PREPARED. THE CHI ENERGY IN THE KITCHEN HAS A GREAT IMPACT ON HOW YOU FEEL AND YOUR ABILITY TO COOK; A BLEND OF METAL, GLASS AND WOOD COMBINE HARMONIOUSLY TO PRODUCE A HEALTHY, POSITIVE CHI.

SOUTH The fire energy in the south increases the risk of feeling over-emotional and having arguments and dramas. Add more soil energy to calm the excess of fire by placing charcoal in small clay containers near to your cooker. Fire energy also does not mix well with the water energy of the sink and you can counter this by keeping plants near the sink – tree energy creates a harmonious flow between fire and water. To boost the tree energy, use wooden surfaces, plants, and the colours green and yellow in your decorative schemes.

SOUTH-WEST AND NORTH-EAST The soil energy of these directions mixes favourably with the fire energy of the cooker but not with the water energy of the sink. This could make it harder to enjoy harmonious family relationships and good health. To better combine the soil and water energies, add more metal energy. A stainless steel sink, a tiled floor, metal pots and pans, the colour white and a metal clock may help.

WEST AND NORTH-WEST The fire energy of the cooker does not mix harmoniously with the metal energy in the west and north-western parts of your home. In addition, the water energy has a slightly draining effect on the metal energy. The result may mean that you find it hard to feel organised and remain focused. To harmonise the fire and metal energy, you need more soil energy. Place

small clay bowls filled with charcoal either side of the hob and oven. Ceramic, limestone or brick floors will help, as will the colour yellow and low-spreading plants. You can also help prevent metal energy from draining away by installing a stainless steel sink and keeping metal objects close to it.

NORTH The water energy of the north becomes excessive when mixed with the water of the sink, and water does not mix well with the fire from the stove. This could lead to a loss of vitality, loneliness and emotional upsets. The solution is to add more tree energy to bring greater harmony between water and fire and drain some of the excessive water energy. Add plenty of plants to your kitchen, use wooden surfaces and the colour green.

OPTIMAL KITCHEN DESIGN

A bright sunny room creates a lively, uplifting place in which to prepare healthy meals. Sunlight also helps keep the kitchen dry and the chi energy fresh and clean. If your kitchen is not bright, use direct lights into the corners of the room. Dark corners are harder to keep clean and chi energy is likely to stagnate here.

Keep the room fresh and alive with plenty of large, leafy plants. These can be used to counteract cutting chi – a fast-flowing form of chi that flows from sharp protrusions; place the

THE CHI ENERGY IN THIS KITCHEN IS METAL, CREATING A FUNCTIONAL ATMOSPHERE. THE FLOW OF ENERGY WILL BE FAST AND ACTIVE, GOOD FOR VITALITY AND ORGANISATION.

plants in front of these corners. The kitchen also needs fresh air, which is essential for chi energy movement and to disperse humidity.

Colours can be used to fine-tune the flow of chi energy. To activate chi energy in your kitchen use yang shades, such as a bright red pot, and to calm the chi energy use yin shades, such as a pastel blue tray. Also consider the five element colours (page 16–17) and see if you can include them in their appropriate location within the room. Try putting bright purple in the fiery south of the room, for example, if you want to make your kitchen more exciting. Use yellow in the south-west if you want to make it more homely.

Wood is the ideal surface for food preparation because it has an organic source and is conducive to a healthy flow of chi energy. Stainless steel creates a more yang, hard, fast-moving atmosphere, which may not be ideal if you spend a reasonable amount of time in the kitchen and need a relaxing atmosphere.

If the kitchen is not in an advantageous location it is particularly important to keep it clean and dry. The most harm comes if chi energy stagnates in the kitchen and influences the health of the food. Dampness and humidity make chi energy heavy and stagnant, so keep surfaces dry. Don't leave food to rot in the kitchen; this radiates an unhealthy chi energy.

SITING APPLIANCES AND SURFACES

When renovating or designing a kitchen, it is important to find the best locations for the stove, sink and work surfaces. They are usually the places where you spend most of your time when you are in a kitchen and, in the case of the stove and sink, they add their own chi energy of fire and water to the room.

Draw the eight directions from the middle of the kitchen using the method on page 21, then use the information below and on the opposite page to find the best site for your cooker, sink and other work surfaces. The only favourable positions for both cooker and sink are the east and south-east directions associated with the tree element, which is harmonious with both fire and water. Certain positions, such as south-west and north-east, can be suitable for the cooker, since fire is harmonious with soil, but other sites will need some Feng Shui solutions.

If your sink is in the south, you need to place plants around it to allow tree energy to combine the fire and water harmoniously. If your cooker is in the south, the fire element will be overpowering and you should calm the area with soil energy, such as by placing ceramic dishes with charcoal around the stove. You need a similar soil remedy if your cooker is in the west or the north-west to counter the clash between the metal energy of these directions and the fire of the stove. If your sink is in the west or north-west, however, you need to prevent the metal from being drained by placing metal objects around the sink, or fitting a stainless steel sink. The north is too quiet for good health and you should place wood and plants around your cooker or sink if it is in this direction. If your cooker or sink is in the south-west or north-east, you should stabilise it with a greater use of metal, such as a metal sink or metallic objects.

your cooking directions

FACING NORTH-EAST This is beneficial for motivation, direction and competitiveness, and would be useful if you want to make a quick meal.

FACING EAST Looking towards the east is good for being active, enthusiastic and busy. It encourages you to focus on getting the details right, although you may feel impatient.

FACING SOUTH-EAST Here you will cook more creative meals. The south-east is favourable for feeling imaginative and artistic, with inspiration for new ideas.

FACING SOUTH This is an outgoing direction, making you feel more passionate about food. However, it is not good for concentration.

FACING SOUTH-WEST This direction is associated with slow, steady progress and practicality, which would be helpful if you needed to pace yourself.

FACING WEST Cooking for pleasure and feeling more content with life results from facing west. It would also be ideal for cooking for fun, although it would not be helpful if you lack motivation or need to concentrate.

FACING NORTH-WEST If you want to feel in control and undertake more responsibility in the kitchen, work facing the north-west. It would also help if you feel that you would like to take your cooking seriously and be more organised.

FACING NORTH This is the most peaceful direction to face while cooking. However, the chi energy of the north is not generally supportive to the amount of activity required to prepare large or creative meals.

USE THE EAST-FACING CHI ENERGY OF THE MORNING SUNSHINE TO BRING ACTIVITY AND ENTHUSIASM TO YOUR COOKING.

kitchen equipment

AVOID USING SYNTHETIC
MATERIALS in the kitchen, such as
plastic work surfaces, vinyl flooring or
nylon carpets, as these interfere with
the natural flow of chi energy.
Electrical equipment, such as
microwave ovens and toasters, create
electrical radiation and disorientate the
natural flow of chi energy. Avoid them
if you can, or place plenty of plants in
the kitchen area to dissipate any
negative energy. Do not use fluorescent
lighting in the kitchen – this type of
light scatters chi energy.

KITCHEN SURFACES Wood is ideal
as it provides a yin surface on which to
prepare your food. It is more receptive
and makes a harmonious relationship
with the yang steel of the knife. Wood
has also been shown to reduce bacterial
infection in food.

THE STOVE This represents the
creation of life, as the food prepared on
the stove literally contributes to the
creation of life in your body. I always
recommend a stove with a natural
flame, such as a gas flame or wood-
burning stove. Avoid electric stoves and
microwave ovens.

WOOD This light,
more yin material is
helpful for adding a
gentle touch to your
cooking. Wood is a
living material with an
ecosystem that
promotes hygienic
cooking.

CERAMIC Ceramic dishes are
more yin than metal and contain
the soil element, providing a
comforting and secure energy.

STAINLESS STEEL
Steel knives and other
utensils are yang. Pots
and pans in stainless
steel are lighter than
enamel, glass or cast
iron dishes and are
therefore slightly more
yin. They are good for
boiling, steaming, stir
frying and thin soups.

GLASS This adds yang energy
to your food, although without
the strength of metal. Glass is
unique as it allows in natural
light, reducing stagnation.

CAST IRON AND
ENAMEL Cast iron has a
powerful yang energy. If it
is coated with enamel to
produce a smooth surface,
it becomes slightly more
yang. Both are suitable
for casseroles, stews and
soups.

COPPER This is a more yin
kind of metal and is useful
when you need to be sensitive
to temperature. Copper pans
are good for delicate sauces.

the healthy ingredients of
feng shui food

THE FOOD YOU EAT HAS A GREATER INFLUENCE on how you feel, your energy levels and your long-term health than virtually every other aspect of your lifestyle. You alone are responsible for choosing a diet that you are confident is healthy – containing the right nutrients and free from harmful ingredients. *Feng Shui Food* offers a philosophy for eating to promote the well-being of your body, your mind and your environment.

Thousands of years before modern nutritionists discovered vitamins and minerals, Asians were using a diet – high in nutrients and fibre, low additives and fat – that is now considered the single greatest factor contributing to the longevity of Eastern populations. *Feng Shui Food* is based on these dietary traditions, providing a nutritional balance for optimum living. The key is to keep a good blend of foods that balance yin and yang and contain all five elements. By following these chi concepts, you will be providing yourself with a healthy diet.

Eastern tradition also prescribes that you eat food with natural chi energy. In the West, the food we eat has changed dramatically in the last 30 years; fresh foods cooked at home have been replaced with pre-cooked, dried, tinned or frozen foods. Sugar, meat and processed food consumption has increased dramatically and, more recently, additives, nuclear irradiation and genetic engineering have altered many of the foods available. Farming

FENG SHUI FOOD FOLLOWS THE HEALTH TRADITIONS OF THE EAST — A DIET OF FRESH, HEALTHY AND NATURAL INGREDIENTS — OFFERING THE BEST PRESCRIPTION FOR A BALANCED, HEALTHY LIFE.

methods, too, have changed; pesticides, chemical fertilisers and factory farming are common. Animals are fed regularly with processed foods, antibiotics and growth hormones. The long-term health effects of these dietary changes is unknown, and *Feng Shui Food* advises that you eat the healthiest and most natural food products you can to safeguard your body. You can do this by choosing organic or home-grown fresh produce where possible, and using traditional fire and stove cooking methods rather than using processed foods and the microwave oven.

SEASONINGS AND FLAVOURINGS

Choosing healthy, natural ingredients is a crucial part of the Eastern diet, and you can avoid additives and processed foods by making your own seasonings and flavourings using the recipes in the appendix (pages 148–155).

For better health, the recipes in this book minimise the use of refined sugars, which can cause health problems by raising the blood-sugar levels too quickly. Instead they use natural sugars, such as maple or rice syrup, which are more nutritious and raise the blood-sugar at a slower rate. Some recipes in Chapter 2 use the natural sweetness of fruit and vegetables, such as pumpkins.

In this book, shoyu sauce is used rather than soy sauce because the former is brewed naturally over a longer period of time using only natural ingredients.

GRAINS

GRAINS, SUCH AS RICE, NOODLES, BREAD AND CEREALS, should make up the main part of your diet. They contain complex carbohydrates, proteins and fats, a range of essential minerals and vitamins, and are high in dietary fibre. Unrefined wholegrains are more nutritious because when the outer husk is broken through refining, the grain begins to oxidise, losing much of its nutritional content over time. Some of the recipes in Chapter 2 use wholegrains, such as rice and barley.

FRUIT & VEG

IT IS IMPORTANT TO EAT A LARGE VARIETY OF FRUIT AND VEGETABLES and to cook them in different ways to give your body the best opportunity for absorbing the nutrients and chi energy that it needs. Beans, pulses, tofu, nuts and seeds are important sources of protein in the East, although every food has protein in order to grow and it would be virtually impossible to design a palatable diet that did not have sufficient protein.

FATS & OILS

FENG SHUI FOOD PREFERS COLD-PRESSED UNSATURATED VEGETABLE OILS, such as olive oil and sesame oil, instead of the unhealthy saturated fats from meat and dairy sources. Saturated fats build up fats in your arteries and around vital organs, increasing the risk of heart and artery disease and cancer.

You can make your own healthy flavoured oils, including basil oil and lemon oil, using the guidelines in the appendix (see page 153).

IN MY OPINION, it is not healthy to drink milk after weaning – after all, no other species on the planet does! The World Health Organisation agrees that consuming milk products increases the risk of heart and artery disease, cancer and asthma. Eggs also are high in saturated fats and raise cholesterol levels in the blood, leading to degenerative illness. Where possible, the recipes in this book use tahini, coconut or soy milk.

FISH & MEAT

HEALTHY, NUTRITIOUS AND LOW IN FAT, fish and seafood feature far more in *Feng Shui Food* than meat. The World Health Organisation has found that eating meat is one of the causes of degenerative illnesses, mostly because it is high in unhealthy saturated fats. Meat also may have traces of growth hormones, antibiotics and toxic residues from the chemicals used to spray the food eaten by the animals. If you want to eat meat, choose healthier organic produce.

EGGS & DAIRY

Every meal you cook can be either more yin or more yang, depending on the ingredients you use and the way you prepare and cook them. This chapter consists of recipes for a variety of yin and yang dishes for each course. All yin recipes appear on the left-hand pages and are matched by similar yang recipes on the right – simply choose the one which best fits in with your mood and health, following the guidelines in Chapter 1. Nothing is completely yin or yang: each dish in this chapter is arranged on the scale below, with those that are significantly yin or yang at either end and the more balanced ones in the middle. All the recipes serve four people.

most yin

2
yin and yang recipes

most yang

mussel and clam soup with orange and coriander

700 g mussels and clams, de-bearded
    and scrubbed

350 ml dry white wine

2 shallots, finely chopped

2 cloves garlic, peeled and chopped

650 ml fish stock (see page 150) or
    water

juice of 3 oranges

1 large bunch fresh coriander,
    chopped

salt and freshly milled black pepper

150 ml crème fraîche or double cream
    (optional)

1 Heat a heavy-based saucepan over a medium-high heat until hot, then drop in the mussels and clams. Pour in the wine and add the shallots, garlic and stock or water. Cover and cook over medium heat for 2–3 minutes.

2 Stir well, then shake the pan to encourage the mussels and clams to open. Add the orange juice, then bring the mixture to the boil. Remove the mussels and clams with a slotted spoon as soon as the liquid reaches boiling point – the majority of them should be opened by now. Set aside.

3 Take the liquid off the heat and pass it through a fine sieve or through muslin, straight into a clean saucepan. Add the chopped coriander, mussels and clams. Taste and then season with salt and pepper (mussels are often very salty and may not need any extra salt). Then stir in the crème fraîche or double cream (optional). Remove and discard any mussels and clams that have not opened. Serve the soup in large shallow bowls.

STEVEN THIS IS ONE OF MY ALL-TIME FAVOURITE SOUPS – the blend of shellfish and oranges makes a delicious and refreshing starter with a heavy dose of character. The mussels and clams in their shells give the dish a sort of moules marinière feeling. Great for an informal dinner, this soup is quick and easy to prepare and the ingredients are all inexpensive. Add the crème fraîche to fuse the flavours together. It makes plenty of soup; enough for 6 starters or 4 hungry people who want second helpings. Eat the shellfish with your fingers and mop up the soup and juices with good, fresh bread (try my bread recipes on pages 154–5).

THE YIN WINE, ORANGE JUICE and coriander counter the yang of the seafood, making this a well-balanced soup. It has more soil and metal chi energy. A perfect dish to strengthen and refresh you on a summer's day, it will also help you to feel more vital, thanks to the shellfish, and can even improve your sex drive!

SIMON

smoked haddock and watercress soup

1 tbsp sunflower oil

2 shallots or 1 small onion, peeled and chopped

1 small fennel bulb, chopped

2 stalks celery, chopped

2 cloves garlic, peeled and finely chopped

250 g smoked haddock, including the bones and skin

1 litre milk

1 large bunch watercress

12 tbsp watercress purée (see page 152)

150 ml crème fraîche

salt and freshly milled black pepper

100 g smoked haddock fillet, flaked and cooked

SMOKED HADDOCK MAKES A WONDERFUL SOUP because it provides an immediate flavour to the stock. By comparison, watercress is delicate but it adds a rounded, soft smoothness to make this soup delectable and sensuous.

STEVEN

THE SMOKED HADDOCK ensures that this is a yang soup – smoked foods being particularly yang – with metal and water energy. Cooking the haddock whole creates a stock high in nutrients and minerals, which makes the soup a good one to eat before you do anything that requires mental concentration or if you'd like to improve your memory.

SIMON

1 Heat the oil in a frying pan over a low heat, then add the shallots, the fennel, the celery and the garlic and cook for 2–3 minutes until tender, stirring all the time. Add the smoked haddock, including the bones and skin. Now cook the mixture for a further 2–3 minutes, stirring constantly and breaking up the fish.

2 Add the milk and bring to a boil. Then reduce the heat and simmer for roughly 15–20 minutes. Take the mixture off the heat and blend the contents of the saucepan in a food processor. Then pour it through a fine

sieve or muslin into a clean saucepan. Put it on a very low heat so it is kept warm but not boiling.

3 Prepare the watercress purée (see page 152) and set aside.

4 Whisk in the crème fraîche and gradually add the watercress purée, salt and pepper. Mix these into the soup thoroughly and set aside.

5 Divide the flaked and cooked haddock fillet into 4 portions. Place 1 portion on each serving bowl. Pour in the soup, and serve immediately.

PUMPKIN IS AN IDEAL VEGETABLE FOR those who have sweet cravings, the sweetness making it a yin dish – and the longer you cook it, the sweeter it becomes. Onions also add a sweetness that increases the longer that they are cooked. The celery, bok choy and tomatoes all are yin but add freshness. Because the soup is a vegetable one, it has a more soothing, yin effect than a meat- or fish-based soup.

The soup would be especially comforting if you suffer from tension, enabling you to feel warmer and more relaxed. Eaten on a regular basis, it will increase the strength of your stomach. It also would help anyone who is trying to reduce his or her sugar consumption as it provides an excellent source of natural sweetness. Because of its sweet taste, pumpkin can increase your intake of the soil element, making you feel more secure and relaxed.

PUMPKIN HAS A COMFORTING, NATURALLY SWEET FLAVOUR and, although pumpkins are particularly good in October, this soup can be served all year round with excellent results – so don't think it's just for Halloween! If you can't get hold of truffle oil, you also can use sesame oil to provide the necessary depth of flavour and character.

STEVEN

pumpkin soup with celery and bok choy

1 tbsp olive oil

1 small onion, peeled and diced

3 cloves garlic, peeled and chopped

2 stalks celery, diced, leaves reserved

1 small fennel bulb, diced

1 litre cold water

300 g pumpkin, peeled and cut into 2 cm cubes

1 tbsp sun-dried tomato paste (see page 152)

salt and freshly milled white pepper

1–2 bok choy leaves (or spinach), finely chopped

2 tomatoes, peeled and chopped into 1 cm cubes

small bunch of fresh basil, finely shredded

1 tsp truffle oil

1 Heat the oil in a pan over a low heat, add the onion, garlic, diced celery and the fennel and cook for 2–3 minutes until the vegetables are tender but not browned.

2 Add the water and pumpkin and bring to the boil. Stir in the tomato paste, then reduce the heat and simmer for 20 minutes until the pumpkin is tender. Season with salt and pepper and remove from the heat. Stir in the celery leaves, the bok choy leaves, the tomatoes and the basil. Drizzle the truffle oil over the soup and then serve.

roasted root vegetable broth
with coriander oil

2½ tbsp olive oil

2 medium carrots, cut into 2 cm pieces

2 medium parsnips, cut into 2 cm pieces

1 medium swede, cut into 2 cm pieces

2 stalks celery, cut into 2 cm pieces

1 squash, cut into 2 cm pieces

6 cloves garlic, peeled

sea salt and freshly milled white pepper

1 tbsp brown rice syrup or honey

1 sprig of thyme

2 small onions, peeled and chopped

200 ml dry white wine

750 ml miso stock (see page 150)

1 tbsp chopped fresh basil

1 tbsp coriander oil (see page 153)

1 Preheat the oven to 200°C. Heat 2 tbsp of the oil in an ovenproof pan over a high heat and add the raw vegetables, 4 whole cloves of garlic, a little salt and pepper, the rice syrup or honey and the thyme. Cook for 1–2 minutes until browned, then transfer to the preheated oven and roast for 20–25 minutes until the vegetables are tender.

2 Meanwhile, heat the remaining oil in a deep saucepan over low heat. Crush the remaining garlic cloves and add to the pan with the onion. Cook for 1–2 minutes until the onion has softened, then add the wine. Increase the heat to medium and cook the mixture until it has reduced to a syrupy consistency.

3 Remove the vegetables from the oven and strain off any excess oil. Discard the thyme. Pour the miso stock into the pan with the onions and bring to a boil. Add the roasted vegetables and simmer for 5 minutes. Then season with salt and pepper to taste and add the chopped basil. Serve in warmed bowls, and drizzle with a little coriander oil.

INSTEAD OF USING A VEGETABLE STOCK as a base, I have used miso (made from cooked soya beans with rice), which adds a really interesting Eastern flavour to this otherwise rustic soup. On a cold winter's day, you can leave the vegetables whole or in large chunks to make this a tasty, warming dish.

STEVEN

ROOT VEGETABLES ARE THE MOST YANG VEGETABLES, and roasting them makes them even more yang, so this is an excellent soup for the winter and colder climates. The thicker the soup, the more yang it will be. Baking the vegetables in oil results in a more rich and satisfying dish. Using miso or shoyu sauce will make it yet more yang; both are also said to be helpful in enriching your blood with minerals while reducing acidity. The overall effect of the soup's sweet and pungent flavours is to increase your soil and metal chi energy.

Eaten on a regular basis this soup will help you to cope better with cold weather while increasing your stamina and endurance.

SIMON

pickled vegetable salad with baby ruby chard and horseradish oil

FOR THE VEGETABLE SALAD

1 carrot, shredded

200 g girolle mushrooms

1 leek, shredded

1 red chilli, deseeded and sliced

1 green chilli, deseeded and sliced

100 g mangetout, shredded

1 bunch mizuno, stalks removed

1 bunch young ruby chard

salt and freshly milled black pepper

2 tbsp horseradish oil (see page 153)

1 large pinch paprika

FOR THE PICKLING JUICES

100 ml wine vinegar

150 ml white wine

1 tbsp rice syrup or honey

1 Place a baking tray in the refrigerator to chill. Pour the pickling juices in a saucepan over a medium heat and add the carrot, mushrooms, leek and chillies. Bring to the boil, then remove from the heat and add the mangetout. Strain the pickling juices and put to one side; these can be reduced to a syrup and used as a salad dressing.

2 Immediately spread the vegetables out on to the chilled tray and chill in the refrigerator until cold, approximately 30–45 minutes.

3 Once the vegetables are chilled, place them in a bowl and toss them with the mizuno leaves and ruby chard. Season to taste with salt and pepper. Divide the salad into 4 equal portions, place on serving plates and drizzle the horseradish oil around the salads. Sprinkle paprika attractively on to the plates, around the edges of the salad, and serve.

THIS IS A DISH THAT TASTES FAR MORE INTERESTING THAN IT SOUNDS. The sweet, tangy flavours of the vegetables spiced with chillies really set your tastebuds on fire. It's a great summer salad, mixed with a variety of summer leaves, and perhaps a few vine tomatoes for good measure.

STEVEN

SIMON

SALADS ARE IN GENERAL RELATIVELY YIN. Fresh, raw, watery salad vegetables are very yin, and wine, vinegar and chilli further enhance the yin energies. Pickling, however, is a yang preparation, and the longer the vegetables are pickled, and the more salty the pickling juice, the more yang they will be. This dish provides greater water and tree chi energy and is very refreshing on a hot day. If it is eaten often, it can encourage you to feel more relaxed.

SIMON

CHARGRILLING THE ASPARAGUS adds fiery yang chi energy to this salad, which results in a very exciting dish. The Parmesan cheese will make the salad even more filling and yang. This is a great dish for social occasions; the fiery quality of the asparagus will encourage people to be more expressive and outgoing. The chi energy of the accompanying salad is more refreshing, light and yin. If you want a more yin salad, replace the Parmesan with grated carrot soaked in shoyu and vinegar.

STEVEN

THE LOVELY SMOKY FLAVOUR of the chargrilled asparagus makes this dish a tasty starter – and chargrilling doesn't overpower its fine texture. In season, asparagus is an excellent vegetable that doesn't need elaborate flavourings, so here we keep it simple but still creative with a dash of lemon oil, or you can also try my garlic oil (see page 153).

chargrilled asparagus salad with olive tapenade

20 spears fresh asparagus
150 ml lemon oil (see page 153)
4 tbsp chopped rocket leaves
4 tbsp chopped lamb's lettuce
2 tbsp chopped baby spinach leaves
1 tbsp chopped coriander leaves
salt and freshly milled
    black pepper
2 tbsp Parmesan cheese shavings
    (optional)
2 tbsp black olive tapenade
    (see page 121)

1 Lower the asparagus spears into a large saucepan of boiling salted water and leave for 1 minute. Remove and plunge them into cold water to refresh them. Drain and place in a bowl.

2 Pour in 100 ml of the lemon oil and marinate the asparagus spears for a minimum of half an hour and a maximum of 24 hours.

3 Place the leaves in a bowl. Remove the asparagus spears from the marinade and trim the thicker ends, to allow quick, uniform cooking, and add the trimmings to the salad.

4 Heat a griddle pan over a high heat until it is very hot, then cook the asparagus spears on it for 1 minute, turning once halfway through cooking. Season with salt.

5 If you are having it, add the Parmesan to the bowl with the salad leaves and toss together. Divide equally between 4 serving plates and drizzle with the remaining lemon oil. Serve the hot asparagus with olive tapenade and freshly milled black pepper.

flash-seared squid salad

4 medium-sized squid, approximately
    10 cm in length

2 tbsp sesame oil

1 bunch mizuno

1 frisée lettuce

1 small bunch young ruby chard

vegetable oil for deep-frying

2 tbsp plain flour seasoned with
    salt and pepper

FOR THE MARINADE

100 ml rice wine vinegar

250 ml rice wine, dry white
    wine or sake

75 ml rice syrup or honey

salt and freshly milled black pepper

juice of 2 limes

1 stick lemongrass, cut into
    3 cm pieces

2 cloves garlic, peeled and sliced

1 red chilli, deseeded and sliced

STEVEN

FLASH-SEARED SQUID IS SUPERBLY TENDER AND TASTY. This delicious salad with marinade gets hotter but better as time goes on. For best results leave for 2 days. With the crisp tentacles served on top, this dish has a unique hot and cold and crisp and soft flavour and texture.

SIMON

SQUID IS A RELATIVELY YIN TYPE OF SEAFOOD and well suited to hot climates where people want to feel cool and refreshed. The salad, vinegar, rice syrup, sake and style of preparation are all cooling. The chilli will encourage heat deep within the body to come to the surface to be dissipated. The more sour vinegar tastes give this dish a greater influence of tree chi energy.

Although it is a generally relaxing dish, the chillies will be stimulating, making it useful for someone who wants to feel revitalised and be more creative and imaginative.

1 Mix together the ingredients for the marinade and set aside. Clean the squid. Remove the tentacles and set aside. Then slice each squid in half so that you have 8 even-sized pieces. Wash thoroughly, then score each slice with a criss-cross pattern using a sharp knife. Cover with the marinade and set aside for at least 1–2 hours.

2 Mix the mizuno, lettuce and chard leaves in a bowl and set aside.

3 Heat the sesame oil in a pan or wok over a high heat. Add the squid and cook for 2–3 minutes until the squid is lightly browned. Take off the heat. Remove the squid with a slotted spoon. Toss the cooked squid through the salad leaves and set aside.

4 Heat the oil for deep-frying. Toss the tentacles in the seasoned flour, then drop them gently into the oil and fry for 2 minutes until crisp. Drain the fried tentacles on a kitchen towel and mix them into the salad to serve.

absolut vodka cured salmon with blood orange juice and lime

16 thin slices raw salmon

2 shallots, finely chopped

1 leek, finely chopped into
   3 mm pieces

2 tbsp Absolut vodka

juice of 1 very ripe blood orange

1 tsp sea salt

freshly milled black pepper

juice of 1 lime

few sprigs mizuno leaves or rocket

1 Lay out the thin slices of salmon on plates – 4 per plate. Sprinkle each plate evenly with the shallots and leek.

2 Mix together the vodka and orange juice, divide into 4 equal portions, and trickle 1 portion on to each plate to cover the salmon.

3 Just before serving, sprinkle lightly with sea salt, freshly ground black pepper and the lime juice. Garnish with mizuno leaves or rocket and serve immediately.

BEING AN ACTIVE FISH, SALMON IS VERY YANG. Its ability to swim upstream means it has a strong and powerful chi energy. The fish is complemented by the vodka, orange and vegetables, all of which are more yin. The vodka is stimulating and gives the salmon a fiery quality. The dish as a whole combines both extremes of yin and yang and would be excellent to eat when you want to feel more inspired. The extremes of yin and yang will activate and broaden your mind, and you may even find that you tend to look at things slightly differently or more creatively after this meal.

SIMON

THIS MAJESTIC AND SLIGHTLY DECADENT DISH IS ONE FOR SPECIAL OCCASIONS. When I first prepared it, I marinated it with the vodka and orange a whole 24 hours before serving. However, I soon discovered that the dressing is so fresh and flavoursome that it needs to be drenched over the salmon only a few minutes before serving to get the benefit of the full flavours and textures.

STEVEN

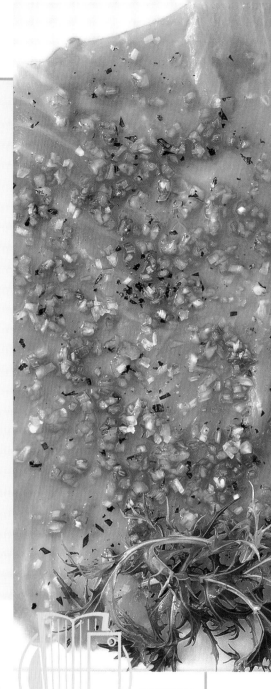

tian of crab

THIS DISH IS IDEAL TO EAT WHEN YOU WANT TO FEEL UPLIFTED AND LIVELY. Although crab meat is comparatively yang, the cucumber, white wine vinegar and coriander all contribute to make this a fresh, yin starter. Its green and white colouring adds to the watery, fresh chi energy, helpful when you need to be more creative.

SIMON

YOU CAN USE CANNED CRAB HERE, but fresh cooked crab meat makes a much more delicious dish. If using fresh crab, first remove all the white meat and then the brown meat from the head. Discard the spongy gills — known as 'dead man's fingers'. You can prepare the pickled cucumber up to two days before serving.

STEVEN

FOR THE CRAB

1 cucumber, thinly sliced lengthwise into 9 cm-long rectangles

3 tbsp white wine vinegar

salt and freshly ground black pepper

1 large cooked cock crab, weighing 1.2–1.3 kg, meat removed, or 600 g canned crab meat

1 tsp ground ginger

2 tbsp crème fraîche

small bunch fresh coriander leaves, chopped, or 1 tbsp dried coriander

1 small cucumber

FOR THE DRESSING

3 tbsp sherry vinegar

3 tbsp extra virgin olive oil

salt and freshly milled black pepper

1 Place the sliced cucumber in a bowl. Add the wine vinegar and salt and pepper to taste, and leave to steep for 30 minutes.

2 Mix the crab, ginger and crème fraîche together, season with salt and black pepper, then add the coriander. Now layer the cucumber with the crab. Place a slice of cucumber on a serving plate, then spoon a layer of crab meat on top, at least 1-cm thick, keeping to the rectangular shape of the cucumber slice. Add another layer of cucumber and then another of crab. Finish with a slice of cucumber. Use a canelle knife to remove a few thin strips of skin from the small cucumber for garnishing. Top each serving with about ½ tbsp of the cucumber skin.

3 To make the dressing, blend the sherry vinegar and olive oil, then season to taste. Drizzle a little dressing on to each tian to serve. You can also use a little voodoo salsa or orange and tomato coulis (both on page 151).

tuna fish cakes

2 large potatoes, peeled and cut into 2 cm cubes

2 red peppers, deseeded and sliced

2 yellow peppers, deseeded and sliced

2 cloves garlic, peeled and roughly chopped

2 tbsp olive oil

salt and freshly milled black pepper

200 g tinned tuna fish, drained

2 egg yolks

6 tbsp fresh breadcrumbs

1 tbsp vegetable oil

small bunch of rocket leaves for garnish

1 Place the cubed potatoes in a saucepan, cover with salted water and bring to the boil. Cook until tender.

2 Preheat the oven to 200°C. Lay the pepper slices on a baking tray, sprinkle with the chopped garlic and drizzle with the olive oil to coat. Season with salt and pepper and bake in the preheated oven (alternatively, grill under high heat) for 15 minutes, until the peppers are soft and tender. Remove the tray from the heat and transfer the contents to a bowl. Cover with clingfilm and set aside until skin peels away.

3 Drain the cooked potatoes and mash them with a little olive oil. Mix together equal amounts of fish and potato in a bowl, season, then mix in the egg yolks. If the mixture is too wet, add a few breadcrumbs. Mould the mixture into 12 small balls. Coat with breadcrumbs.

4 Heat the vegetable oil in a frying pan over low heat. Place the fish cakes in the pan and cook for 5 minutes until browned, turning the cakes from time to time. Meanwhile, arrange the peppers into neat piles in the centre of each serving plate. Place 3 fish cakes on top of each pepper pile, drizzle with a little olive oil, garnish with a few torn rocket leaves and serve.

FOR A FISH CAKE, you don't strictly need to go to the expense of fresh tuna. This quick and easy dish takes only a few minutes to prepare (except for the peppers), makes a great starter and can also make a satisfying main meal for all the family. I like to serve this with a dash of voodoo salsa or orange and tomato coulis (both on page 151).

STEVEN

TUNA, A YANG FISH, aids strength and vitality and, with the addition of salt, egg yolks and baking, it creates a strong yang dish. The red of the peppers gives the food an exciting look, and the mixture of the richness with the garlic makes it a dish that can help you to feel more dynamic. The chi energy will increase your determination and strengthen your resolve.

SIMON

oriental pickled vegetable wonton rolls

SIMON

THE LIGHTLY COOKED VEGETABLES, together with the wine, rice syrup and vinegar, make this a yin dish. Shiitake mushrooms and grated mooli or radish are particularly yin and can help reduce fats in the blood – which helps to counteract the effects of deep-frying. The most powerful element in this dish is tree.

ONCE YOU HAVE DISCOVERED THE THINGS YOU CAN DO with a wonton wrapper, you can play! Try experimenting with all sorts of fillings – duck, chicken, tofu, beansprouts and tiger prawns all work well.

STEVEN

2 small onions, peeled and finely shredded
900 g shiitake mushrooms, finely shredded
8 tbsp beansprouts, finely shredded
1 large bunch bok choy or spinach, shredded
1 large bunch coriander, stalks removed and finely shredded
8 spring onions, finely shredded
8 wonton wrappers, 10 x 10 cm
1 egg white, beaten
vegetable oil for deep-frying
2 tbsp sesame oil
2 heaped tsp sesame seeds
2 tbsp grated mooli or radish to serve
8 tbsp shoyu sauce for dipping

FOR THE PICKLING JUICES
100 ml white wine vinegar
150 ml white wine
100 ml rice syrup or honey

1 Place the pickling juices in a saucepan and bring to the boil. Drop in the onions, mushrooms and bean sprouts and return to the boil; then remove the pan from the heat. Allow to sit for 3 minutes to cool a little, then drop in the bok choy and coriander.

2 Remove the vegetables using a slotted spoon and spread on a baking tray. Chill in the refrigerator for 10 minutes.

3 Once the vegetables are chilled, remove them from the refrigerator and place them in a bowl. Add the spring onions and mix well.

4 Spread out the wonton wrappers on a clean surface and, using a pastry brush, coat the edges with egg white. Turn one of the wrappers so that one of its corners is pointing towards you. Take ½ tbsp of the chilled vegetable mixture and spoon this on to the middle of the wrapper. Lift up the corner nearest you, curl it over the filling. Next fold the left and right corners of the wrapper in towards the centre. Then, roll up the wonton by pushing the roll away from you. Make sure you roll it tightly. Repeat with the remaining 7 wrappers.

5 Heat the vegetable oil in a deep-fat fryer to 175ºC. Deep-fry the filled wonton for approximately 2 minutes, until browned. Remove the fried wontons. Brush each one with a little sesame oil and sprinkle with sesame seeds while still warm. Serve immediately, with grated mooli and shoyu, or cut in half and serve as canapés with chive stalks, as pictured.

smoked salmon sushi rolls

4 slices smoked salmon, weighing roughly 100 g each

1 tsp wasabi paste (see page 149)

5 tbsp glutinous rice or risotto rice

1 tbsp rice wine vinegar

1 sheet nori seaweed, 24 x 16 cm

1 tbsp shoyu sauce

salt and freshly milled black pepper

4 tsp salmon keta or caviar to serve

few sprigs mizuno or chervil, trimmed

1 Spread out a length of clingfilm to 30 x 30 cm. Arrange the slices of smoked salmon on the clingfilm in single layer so that they form a neat rectangle, approximately 15 x 25 cm. Spread the wasabi paste over the salmon, and then refrigerate while you prepare the rice.

2 Put the rice in a saucepan and cover with salted water (approximately 250 ml). Add the rice vinegar. Bring to the boil and continue to boil over a medium heat until the rice has absorbed all the liquid. Take the pan off the heat and leave to cool. If the rice absorbs all the water but remains uncooked, add a little more water – approximately 50 ml; but do not saturate the rice or it will not stick together. Allow the rice to rest in the saucepan for at least 10 minutes.

3 Cover the smoked salmon with the sheet of nori seaweed. Brush with shoyu sauce to soften the seaweed. Once the rice is cooled, spoon a layer over half the seaweed, along one of the long edges. Then roll the layers up together, starting at the long edge with the rice spread along it. Make sure you roll tightly. Keep the roll in the clingfilm to help it maintain its shape, then chill in the refrigerator for a minimum of 1 hour.

4 Once chilled, slice the roll into 8 mini rolls, each one roughly 3 cm long. Place two rolls on each plate, turning the rolls so that they stand with the filling facing upwards. Top each one with ½ tsp salmon keta or caviar and a trimmed sprig of mizuno or chervil to serve. You can place small dishes with shoyu sauce, wasabi paste and pickled mooli (see page 149) on the plate for dipping. This recipe makes approximately 8 little sushi rolls; simply multiply all the ingredients if you would like to make more.

SUSHI SHOULD BE ALIVE WITH A FRESH AND ZINGY TASTE. The shoyu and wasabi add an extra richness. Each mouthful should be a balance of spice, texture and flavour, all in one small, compact, individual portion. Traditionally, the Japanese use bamboo mats to roll the sushi, but I find clingfilm easier.

STEVEN

SALMON IS ITSELF AN ACTIVE YANG FISH, and the nori seaweed and shoyu contribute to make this a more yang dish. The wasabi paste adds metal chi energy and is used to help make the fish more digestible. Japanese sushi chefs believe that wasabi is an essential accompaniment to raw fish.

SIMON

steamed cod with bok choy and yellow squash coulis

FOR THE SQUASH COULIS

1 tsp saffron threads

1 large butternut squash, peeled,
   chopped and with seeds removed

100 ml clear vegetable stock
   (see page 150)

1 tbsp rice syrup or honey

1 level tsp ground nutmeg

salt and freshly milled black pepper

FOR THE COD AND COURGETTES

4 x 175 g cod fillets, skinned

8 large leaves bok choy or spinach

2 large yellow or green courgettes

3 tbsp olive oil

1 To make the squash coulis, heat 250 ml water in a saucepan to just below boiling, then add the saffron and squash. Poach the squash for 5–7 minutes until tender. Remove using a slotted spoon and place in a food processor. Blend to a smooth purée, then pass through a fine sieve. Mix in the heated vegetable stock, rice syrup and nutmeg. Season and set aside, keeping warm.

2 To prepare the cod, heat some water in a pan and simmer, then sit a steamer basket on top, ensuring that it does not touch the water. Wrap the cod with the bok choy, place it in the basket, season with salt and steam gently for 8–10 minutes. (Alternatively, bake the fish in 150 ml white wine at 200°C for 10–12 minutes.) Remove from the steamer and keep warm.

3 Use a canelle knife to cut fine strips of skin from the courgettes, then slice the courgettes diagonally. Heat the olive oil in a frying pan over a medium-high heat. Add the slices and fry for 30 seconds; add the strips and fry for a further 30 seconds. Season with salt.

4 Place the courgette slices on each plate, sit the wrapped cod on top, then garnish with the strips of courgette. Taste the squash coulis and season appropriately. Pour it around the courgette slices and serve.

STEVEN

THE BOK CHOY WRAP is a great way of serving and seasoning fish. Place vine tomatoes or mushrooms under the bok choy as an alternative. The sauce – made with squash, a little rice syrup and nutmeg – adds amazing flavours and colours to the delicate taste of the cod.

SIMON

COD IS YIN, as are courgettes and bok choy, and together they create an exquisite yin main course. The light steaming process is also a yin preparation, making the dish uplifting and revitalising, full of energy without being too heavy. The squash adds a richness, while retaining the yin energy.

poached wild salmon with saffron-infused mussel sauce

FOR THE SAUCE

1 tsp olive oil

2 shallots, peeled and chopped

2 cloves garlic, peeled and chopped

1 level tsp saffron threads

450 g mussels, de-bearded and
   scrubbed

150 ml dry white wine

125 g chilled unsalted butter, cut
   into 2 cm cubes

salt and freshly milled black pepper

FOR THE SALMON AND SPINACH

500 ml fish stock (see page 150)

3 pieces star anise

4 x 125 g wild salmon steaks

½ tbsp sunflower oil

225 g spinach

salt

1 pinch freshly ground nutmeg

4 tbsp chopped oven-dried tomatoes
   (see page 152)

1 For the sauce, heat the oil in a large pan over a low heat then add the shallots, garlic, saffron, mussels and wine and cook for 5–7 minutes, stirring continuously. Cover with a lid and simmer for 2–3 minutes.

2 Remove the mussels with a slotted spoon and discard. Whisk in the chilled butter. Season the sauce if necessary, cover, then set aside.

3 Place the fish stock and star anise in a saucepan and bring to the boil, then add the salmon steaks. Reduce the heat to just below boiling and poach the salmon for 2 minutes, then turn the

fish over and poach for a further 2 minutes. Remove the salmon using a slotted spoon and set aside. I always store the poaching liquor for future use.

4 Heat the sunflower oil in a frying pan or wok over a medium heat, then add the spinach leaves. Toss in the

hot oil for 1 minute until wilted. Season with salt and a pinch of nutmeg and remove from the heat. Divide the leaves into 4 portions and make a bed of the leaves on each plate. Place the salmon on the spinach. Cover the fish with the warm oven-dried tomatoes, spoon over the warm sauce and serve.

THE YANG SALMON AND THE YANG SHOYU flavouring make this a dish for strength and vitality. The tomatoes are oven-dried to add more hearty yang energy. The wine and vegetables provide some refreshing yin energy. The cooking style gives the dish a greater amount of water and tree energy.

SIMON

WILD SALMON IS VERY DIFFERENT from farmed salmon. It has a silky, delicate flavour and needs careful cooking; poaching or steaming is ideal. Farmed salmon has an earthier flavour and if you are using it, leave the mussels in the sauce and pour it over for a *pot au feu* style dish.

STEVEN

poached pigeon, cider-braised cabbage and port reduction

1.4 litres chicken stock
   (see page 150)
2 pieces star anise
1 small bunch wild thyme
1 large cabbage, finely shredded
400 ml dry cider
2 apples, peeled, cored and
   chopped into 1 cm dice
1 tbsp fennel seeds
4 squab pigeons
salt and freshly milled
   black pepper
150 ml port
vegetable oil for deep-frying
2 small beetroot, finely shredded and
   deep fried (see page 149)

1 Heat the stock in a large saucepan over a medium heat. Add the star anise and thyme and bring to the boil. Skim with a small strainer and keep warm.

2 Preheat the oven to 170°C. Place the cabbage in a deep-sided oven-proof dish and cover with cider and apples. Add 400 ml of the chicken stock and the fennel seeds. Cook in the preheated oven for 1 hour.

3 Meanwhile, remove and discard the squabs' legs and season inside and outside the birds. Drop into the saucepan with the reserved stock and simmer for 7 minutes. Remove the squab, place in a bowl, cover and allow to rest. Set the stock aside.

4 Strain the cooked cabbage and place it in a bowl. Put the cooking liquor in a saucepan and reduce over medium-high heat until it has the consistency of syrup. Pour it over the cabbage, season the mixture to taste and set aside.

5 For the sauce, remove 250 ml of the stock, place in a pan and reduce until halved in quantity. Add the port and reduce for 5 minutes until it is the consistency of syrup.

Place the squab in the remaining stock over a high heat, cover and poach for 2 minutes. Remove the squab, which should be medium to rare, and separate the breasts. Add a little cabbage to the plates and place 2 breasts on top of each. Pour the port sauce around the meat and serve topped with fried beetroot shreds.

barbecued duck breast with mango and black bean sauce

FOR THE MARINADE

1 tbsp tomato ketchup

100 ml white wine vinegar

150 ml white wine

150 ml olive oil

handful of coriander stalks, chopped

FOR THE DUCK AND SAUCE

4 x 175–200 g duck breasts

100 ml hoi sin sauce

50 g drained, fermented black beans

200 ml red wine

400 ml chicken stock (see page 150)

250 g rice noodles, preblanched

1 tbsp sesame oil

1 bunch fresh sage leaves

1 red and 1 green chilli, deseeded

½ tbsp coriander seeds

juice of 2 limes

1 mango, peeled and diced

1 Mix the ketchup, vinegar and white wine in a saucepan and whisk in the olive oil. Place over a high heat, bring to the boil, then stir in the coriander. Take off the heat. Once the marinade is cold, place the duck breasts in a bowl and pour the marinade over the duck. Cover and leave in the refrigerator to marinate for at least 2 hours and at most 24 hours.

2 Preheat the oven to 200°C. Mix the hoi sin sauce and the black beans in a bowl. Set aside. Bring the red wine and stock to the boil in a pan and simmer for 15–25 minutes until it has a coating consistency. Reduce the heat and stir in the black bean mixture. Keep warm on a low heat while you prepare the duck breasts.

3 Heat a griddle pan until red hot. Transfer the duck breasts to the griddle and cook for 2 minutes on both sides. Remove from the heat, place in a warmed baking tray, skin-side down, and roast in the oven for 5–7 minutes. Remove from the oven, leave to rest for 2 minutes, then cut each breast in half.

4 Heat the sesame oil in a wok over a high heat, then add the noodles, half the sage leaves and chillies, and all of the coriander seeds and lime juice. Stir-fry for 1–2 minutes. Divide the mixture into 4 portions on serving plates. Stir the remaining chillies and sage leaves with the mango into the sauce. Put the duck halves on the noodles. Pour over the black bean sauce and serve.

moroccan chicken with coconut crust

FOR THE CRUST

4 tbsp fresh breadcrumbs

2 tbsp chopped fresh parsley

½ tbsp cumin seeds

4 tbsp desiccated coconut

85 g unsalted butter

salt and freshly milled black pepper

FOR THE COULIS

1 tbsp olive oil

2 shallots, peeled and chopped

3 cloves garlic, peeled and crushed

150 ml white wine

1.8 kg ripe tomatoes, quartered

3 oranges, peeled and chopped

2 red chillies, deseeded and sliced

salt and freshly milled black pepper

FOR THE COUSCOUS

250 g couscous

1 tsp allspice or Chinese five spice

1 tsp ground ginger

1 green chilli, deseeded and shredded

300 ml chicken stock (see page 150)

FOR THE CHICKEN

1 tbsp olive oil

salt and freshly milled black pepper

4 x 175–200 g chicken breasts,
    skinned

1 Place the breadcrumbs, parsley, cumin seeds, coconut and butter in a food processor and blend to a mouldable 'dough'. Season to taste and set aside. Then make the coulis. Heat the oil over a low heat. Add the shallots, garlic and cook for 2 minutes, then add the wine, tomatoes, oranges and chillies and simmer for 30 minutes.

2 Meanwhile, mix the couscous with the spices, ginger and chilli in a heatproof bowl. Bring the stock to the boil in a small saucepan, then pour it into the bowl with the couscous. Leave to stand for 10 minutes until the couscous has absorbed all the liquid.

3 Preheat the oven to 200ºC. Heat the olive oil in a large frying pan over a high heat. Season the chicken, and fry in the oil for 2 minutes on each side.

Transfer to a baking tray and roast in the oven for 10 minutes.

4 Take the coulis off the heat, pour into a liquidizer and purée. Pass through a sieve, season and set aside.

5 Remove the chicken from the oven and leave until cool enough to handle. Press a thick coating of the 'dough' on to each chicken breast. Return to the oven for 4–5 minutes. Heap the couscous on to plates. Place 1 breast on top of each mound of couscous. Pour the sauce around the couscous and serve.

CHICKEN, COUSCOUS AND TOMATOES ARE are all more yin choices of meat, grain and vegetable. Use shelled tiger prawns or langoustines instead of chicken to make the dish even more yin.

SIMON

THE CRUST IS QUICK AND EASY TO MAKE and gives the chicken a lift of interesting flavours, complementing the spicy coulis and the bed of soft couscous.

STEVEN

wild venison with potato towers

FOR THE SAUCE

150 ml game stock (see page 150)

100 ml red wine

½ tbsp cardamom pods

juice of 1 orange

FOR THE POTATOES

1 kg potatoes, peeled

2 egg yolks

salt and freshly milled black pepper

3 tbsp plain flour

1 egg, beaten with a dash of milk

8 tbsp fresh white breadcrumbs

vegetable oil for deep-frying

FOR THE VENISON

1 tbsp grape seed or light olive oil

4 x 175–200 g wild venison steaks

salt and freshly milled black pepper

FOR THE CABBAGE

**1 medium-sized green or savoy
    cabbage**

1 tbsp olive oil

1 tsp truffle oil

salt and freshly milled black pepper

1 Make the game stock (see page 150) a day in advance so it may set. Use a scraper to skim off the fat.

2 Boil the potatoes in salted water for 20 minutes until just tender. Drain and mash. Stir in the yolks, and season. Mould into 4 triangles. Dust with flour, brush with egg wash, and coat in bread crumbs. Chill for at least 10 minutes.

3 Boil the stock, wine and cardamom pods. Simmer until reduced by a third, then take off the heat, stir in the orange juice and set aside.

4 Preheat oven to 220ºC. Heat 1 tbsp oil over a medium heat. Cook the venison for 1 minute on each side. Season and transfer to the oven for 5–7 minutes until medium-rare.

5 Plunge the cabbage leaves into boiling water for 30 seconds, then into cold water. Heat the olive and truffle oils in a wok. Stir-fry the leaves for 1 minute. Season and drain. Next, heat the vegetable oil in a deep-fryer to 170ºC. Deep-fry the potato triangles for 2–3 minutes. Take the venison out of the oven, rest for 1 minute, then cut each steak into 3–4 slices. Serve on the cabbage leaves with a potato triangle per serving. Strain the sauce, pour around the venison and serve.

A SADDLE OF WILD VENISON is lean, tender and flavoursome. It needs little handling: just gently roast it, leaving it pink and juicy, medium to rare. Try to get wild meat; farmed venison is more mealy and not so full flavoured.

VENISON COMES FROM AN ACTIVE, yang animal, and the egg and salt combine to make this a hearty yang dish. The wine, orange and vegetables add a yin element. The fact that venison is from a wild animal gives it a more healthy chi energy than meat from animals farmed in unnatural conditions.

STEVEN

SIMON

lasagna of spinach pasta with forest mushrooms and pimento oil

450 g assorted wild and forest mushrooms

115 g shiitake mushrooms

½ tbsp light olive oil

3 shallots, finely chopped

3 cloves garlic, peeled and
 chopped

75 ml Madeira or any dry
 sherry

2 tbsp finely chopped
 tarragon

salt and freshly milled
 black pepper

225 g fromage frais

12 sheets spinach pasta,
 cut to 13 x 7.5 cm
 rectangles, cooked

1 tbsp extra virgin olive oil

4 tbsp Parmesan cheese shavings

2 tbsp pimento oil (see page 153)

STEVEN

FOREST MUSHROOMS OR WILD MUSHROOMS? I use some of each and choose carefully, depending on what's available at the time. Some wild mushrooms are tasty but extremely expensive and some forest mushrooms are farmed, have less flavour, but are far cheaper. A few dried mushrooms, such as porcini, can enhance the flavour – use half the quantity of fresh mushrooms and soak in warm water for 10–15 minutes.

MUSHROOMS ARE ONE OF THE MOST YIN VEGETABLES and Madeira, too, is yin, combining to make a light yin pasta dish. You can make it even more yin by adding grated carrot marinated in vinegar for 2 hours instead of Parmesan cheese. In terms of the five elements it has more tree energy.

SIMON

1 Pick through the mushrooms and remove any dirt, needles, etc. Wipe the mushrooms with a damp cloth – do not wash them with water, as this will wash away some flavour. Slice the larger mushrooms in half.

2 Heat the light olive oil in a large frying pan over a low heat. Place the shallots and garlic in the pan and cook for 1 minute, then add the mushrooms. Cook for a further 2–3 minutes, tossing the contents of the pan occasionally to prevent sticking.

3 Now add the sherry. Stir well and throw in the chopped tarragon, salt and black pepper. Remove the pan from the heat and allow to cool for roughly 1–2 minutes before stirring in the fromage frais.

4 Place the pasta in a pan of boiling salted water with 1 tbsp extra virgin olive oil and heat for 2 minutes. Drain the pasta thoroughly.

5 Divide the pasta into 4 portions. Layer the pasta with the mushroom mixture on plates, beginning and ending with a layer of pasta. Place a little parmesan in the centre of the top layer of each serving, then melt it under a hot grill for 2 minutes. Drizzle with pimento oil, sprinkle with freshly milled black pepper and serve.

tempura tofu hot pot with shoyu and somen noodles

750 ml clear vegetable stock (see page 150)

100 ml shoyu

1 tbsp hoi sin sauce

1 tsp grated ginger

115 g dried somen noodles

4 spring onions, halved

1 red chilli, deseeded and sliced

1 green chilli, deseeded and
  sliced

150 g shiitake mushrooms,
  sliced

3 tbsp pickled carrots
  leeks and peppers
  (see page 149)

freshly milled black
  pepper

FOR THE TEMPURA TOFU

2 egg whites

juice of 1 lemon

2 tbsp cornflour, sifted

salt and freshly milled black
  pepper

vegetable oil for deep-frying

225 g tofu, cut into 2.5 cm cubes

few leaves fresh coriander or flat-leaf parsley (optional)

little water until the batter is thickened to coating consistency. Season. Heat some vegetable oil in a pan or deep-fat fryer to 175°C. Dip each of the tofu pieces into the batter, then drop them gently into the hot oil and cook for 1–2 minutes until golden. Remove and drain. Ladle the hot pot into four large, flat 'soup style' serving bowls. Add the tofu and coriander or parsley leaves (optional) and serve.

SITTING ON TOP OF THE HOT POT, THE TOFU SHOULD BE CRISP to offer a variety of textures. The flavour of the liquid should be slightly sweet but spicy – you can use miso stock if you prefer (see page 150). As an alternative, try the same hot pot with poached or steamed fish.

STEVEN

1 Bring the vegetable stock to the boil and add the shoyu, hoi sin sauce and ginger. Then add the noodles and boil for 4–6 minutes until the noodles are reconstituted.

2 Add the spring onions, chillies, mushrooms, the pickled vegetables and some pickling juice. Simmer for 3–4 minutes, then season with black pepper. Taste the mixture at this point – if the shoyu that you are using comes through a little too salty, add 100 ml red wine to knock it back. Remove from the heat, cover to keep warm and set aside.

3 For the tempura, beat the egg whites until semi-stiff and fold in the lemon juice. Whisk in the cornflour and add a

THIS MORE YANG DISH IS NOURISHING AND WARMING. Japanese somen noodles are made from buckwheat, grown in harsh climates, and these are therefore the most yang type of noodle. Pickled vegetables add another yang element; the longer they are pickled, the more yang they become. The more spicy you make this dish, the more fiery it becomes. Add a pinch of grated ginger to the dish before serving to make it more revitalising.

SIMON

VOODOO SALSA IS ONE OF MY BEST
DISCOVERIES, comprising an exotic combination of
chillies, tomatoes, mangoes and spices. Goat's cheese is
a personal favourite, but you can also use blue cheese
or even Parmesan if you prefer.

CORIANDER, LIGHT OLIVE OIL AND
VOODOO SALSA are all yin ingredients. The
boiling and frying processes are more yin than
baking or braising, providing a quick energy that,
if taken regularly, can improve your endurance
and stamina. This dish will have a reasonably even
mixture of each kind of five element chi energy. The
mix of ingredients makes it perfect for a light meal,
a snack or even a packed lunch.

SIMON

risotto cakes with goat's cheese and voodoo salsa

3 tbsp light olive oil

200 g pancetta, chopped

3 shallots, peeled and finely chopped

2 cloves garlic, peeled and finely chopped

450 g Carnaroli or Arborio risotto rice

1.4 litres clear vegetable stock (see page 150) or water

1 bunch fresh coriander, chopped

salt and freshly milled black pepper

2 heaped tbsp tahini

225 g grated English goat's cheese

2 eggs, beaten

300 g fresh breadcrumbs

4 tbsp voodoo salsa (see page 151)

1 Line a baking tray (30 x 20 x 2.5 cm) with grease-proof paper and set aside. Heat 1 tbsp of the oil in a heavy-based saucepan over a medium heat. Add the pancetta, shallots and garlic and cook until just tender. Stir in the rice. Meanwhile, heat the stock to simmering. Add a ladle-full of stock to the pan and allow the rice to absorb it before adding another. Stir frequently. Continue until the rice has swollen and all the stock is absorbed.

2 Stir the coriander into the pan, season with salt and black pepper, then remove from the heat and fold in the tahini, followed by half the goat's cheese. Pour into the baking tray and level out the surface using the back of a spoon. Set in the refrigerator for 2 hours, then use a 7 cm diameter circular metal cutter to cut out 8 circles. Brush both sides of each circle with beaten egg, then turn in fresh breadcrumbs to coat thoroughly.

3 Preheat the oven to 200°C. Heat the remaining oil in a frying pan over a medium heat. Fry the cakes until they are golden, for 1 minute on each side, then place on a baking tray in a preheated oven for 5–6 minutes to ensure that the centres are heated. Preheat a hot grill. Sprinkle the cakes with goat's cheese and glaze under the grill. Serve with voodoo salsa.

braised rice in red wine with baby pumpkin

2½ tbsp light olive oil

2 baby pumpkins, deseeded and halved

1 red pepper, deseeded and sliced

2 cloves garlic, peeled and crushed

1 red onion, peeled and thinly sliced

450 g brown rice

150 ml clear vegetable stock (see page 150) or
    boiling water

300 ml red wine

salt and freshly milled black pepper

1 Preheat the oven to 200°C. Use ½ tbsp olive oil to brush inside the pumpkin halves and along the rims. Cover with foil and bake in the preheated oven for 1½ hours, until the flesh is tender. Then remove from the oven and keep warm until the rice is prepared.

2 While the pumpkin is cooking, heat the remaining 2 tbsp of oil in a casserole over a medium heat, then add the pepper, garlic and onion. Cook the vegetables until tender. Then turn the oven temperature down to 150°C.

3 Reduce the heat under the casserole to low and add the rice, the vegetable stock (or water) and half of the red wine. Season with salt to taste, cover with a lid and transfer to the preheated oven and cook for 20 minutes.

4 Remove from the the oven, stir in the remaining red wine then return to the oven for a further 15 minutes. Take the casserole out of the oven and leave to rest on top of the stove, allowing the rice to absorb the wine fully. Place each pumpkin half on a serving plate. Spoon some rice on to the the centre of each pumpkin half and serve immediately.

STEVEN

BAKING OR ROASTING A PUMPKIN gives it a sweet, soft flavour, delicious for enriching the more savoury rice. I have cooked the braised rice in loads of red wine, and the end product is rich and sensational. This is a fabulous accompaniment to an uplifting winter's dinner party.

SIMON

EXCEPT FOR THE PEPPER AND WINE, THE INGREDIENTS of this recipe are more yang. Brown rice is a yang grain, and baking it further increases the yang – the longer it is baked, the more yang it becomes. This is a good dish for the winter to help you to build up your resistance to seasonal colds.

In terms of the five elements, this more condensed dish will have a greater degree of metal chi energy.

tempura of vegetables with shoyu dip

FOR THE VEGETABLES

1 carrot, peeled

8 cauliflower or broccoli florets

8 sticks baby sweetcorn

1 red pepper

1 tsp nutmeg

1 tsp allspice

1 tsp ground ginger

1 tsp freshly milled black pepper

vegetable oil for deep-frying

FOR THE TEMPURA BATTER

2 egg whites

juice of 1 lemon

2 tbsp cornflour

salt and freshly milled black pepper

FOR DIPPING SAUCE

50 ml shoyu

1 tsp rice wine vinegar

1 tsp grated ginger

1 red chilli, deseeded and finely
    chopped (optional)

1 green chilli, deseeded and finely
    chopped (optional)

1 tsp grated mooli or radish

1 Cut the carrot into strips, 7 cm long and 1 cm thick. Plunge the carrot, cauliflower and sweetcorn into a pan of boiling salted water for 2 minutes until just tender. Refresh in cold water, drain, place in a bowl and set aside. Cut the pepper in the same way as the carrot and add to the bowl. Add the nutmeg, allspice, ground ginger and pepper, and toss to coat the vegetables.

2 For the batter, beat the egg white until semi-stiff and fold in the lemon juice. Whisk in cornflour and a little water until thickened and season.

3 Heat the vegetable oil in a wok or deep-fat fryer to 175ºC. Dip 4 or 5 of the vegetable pieces into the batter and place them in the oil gently. Cook for 2 minutes until golden, then remove with a slotted spoon, drain on kitchen paper, then repeat the process until all the vegetables are battered and cooked.

4 Mix all the ingredients for the dipping sauce, reserving the mooli to be placed on top. Serve in a small bowl in the centre of a large plate with the warm tempura of vegetables arranged around the dipping sauce.

STEVEN

EVERYONE LOVES TEMPURA – the crisp vegetables with spicy shoyu dip give great character and style to what is basically a plate of lightly cooked vegetables! Try any sort of vegetable you wish; I like to use slices of red pepper to add some extra colour.

SWEETCORN AND CAULIFLOWER are both yin vegetables, and the quick cooking method of tempura is also yin, keeping the vegetables fresh and retaining their nutrients. Grated mooli is used to help make the oil more digestible while grated ginger improves blood circulation. It is a good dish to improve energy movement around the body, warming the extremities and relaxing the inner body.

SIMON

SIMON

CABBAGE IS A HARDY YANG VEGETABLE.
The longer it is cooked, the more yang it becomes,
especially if you braise it in the oven. Salt will make
it yet more yang, so avoid adding too much. The yin
raisins and vinegar will help to counter this. The
sweet and sour tastes add more soil and tree chi
energy respectively.

Braised cabbage is one of the ideal winter
vegetable dishes that can help you to become more
hardy and resistant to cold weather.

THOSE WHO DISLIKE CABBAGE WILL BE
SURPRISED at how you can make it so delicious (it is, after
all, one of the most nutritious vegetables). The raisins and
cinnamon add an extra flavour but don't affect the texture of the
cabbage. The sweet and sour combination is one of my favourites,
but make sure that this tasty side vegetable doesn't compete with
your main dish.

STEVEN

sweet and sour braised cabbage **with raisins and cinnamon**

1 medium-sized green cabbage
1 tsp freshly grated nutmeg
3 tbsp white wine vinegar
55 g sultanas or raisins
1 tsp ground cinnamon
2 tbsp barley malt or honey
350 ml clear vegetable stock
   (see page 150)
salt and freshly milled black pepper

1 Preheat the oven to 150°C. Peel off any tough or damaged leaves from the cabbage and remove the core while keeping the cabbage whole. Shred the cabbage into strips, approximately 1 cm wide and as long as possible, and place the strips in a baking dish. Mix in the nutmeg, vinegar, sultanas, cinnamon and barley malt or honey.

2 Bring the stock to the boil in a saucepan, then pour it into the baking dish to cover the cabbage. Season with salt and cover with tin foil. Place the dish in the preheated oven and cook for 30 minutes, stirring from time to time. Remove the baking dish from the oven and sprinkle the cabbage with black pepper to serve.

IN ADDITION TO THE VEGETABLES, MINT AND SYRUP, the quick cooking style makes this a yin dish. Tahini is high in minerals, and using it is a healthier and more yin way to make a dish creamy. The light freshness of this dish generates slightly more tree chi energy. Serve on a hot day or whenever you want to feel more light hearted and easy going. It can also be useful if you want to be more creative or imaginative.

SIMON

THE CRUNCH OF FRESH PEAS is unbeatable, but quality organic frozen peas are next best if you can't get hold of the real thing. I have lightened up this recipe by leaving out any butter, flour or milk, and instead using tahini to give the dish a creamy but healthy and light background flavour – perfect as a vegetable accompaniment to fish or meat.

STEVEN

petits pois à la française

500 ml clear vegetable stock (see page 150)
1 tbsp light vegetable oil, such as sunflower oil
8 small shallots, peeled and finely chopped
900 g fresh or frozen peas
150 ml light tahini or double cream
few sprigs fresh mint
4 heaped tbsp chopped Romaine lettuce leaves
1 tbsp honey
salt and freshly milled black pepper

1 Heat the vegetable stock to simmering over medium heat. Then heat the oil in a large saucepan over a low heat, add the shallots and cook for 1–2 minutes until tender. Pour in the hot stock and peas and simmer for 5 minutes.

2 Mix the tahini or cream into the pan, stir in the mint and lettuce, then take the pan off the heat. Add the honey and season with salt and pepper to taste. Serve immediately.

thyme roasted root vegetables

2 medium-sized carrots
1 medium-sized parsnip
1 medium-sized turnip or swede
1 medium-sized fennel bulb
4 cloves garlic
1 tbsp vegetable or grape seed oil
1 fresh sprig of thyme
½ tbsp rice syrup or honey
salt and freshly milled black pepper
100 ml dry white wine

1 Preheat the oven to 200°C. Peel the vegetables and cut into rustic chunks, approximately 5 cm long and 2 cm thick. Leave the cloves of garlic in their skins.

2 Heat the oil in an ovenproof frying pan over medium-high heat and fry the vegetables until slightly browned. Add the sprig of thyme and rice syrup and stir well. Season with salt and pepper to taste, then add the wine.

3 Transfer the pan to the preheated oven and roast the vegetables for 20 minutes, stirring and tossing them occasionally to prevent them from sticking to the pan.

4 Take the pan out of the oven then remove the vegetables using a slotted spoon. Transfer them to a warmed serving platter, garnish with the sprig of thyme that was used during cooking and serve immediately.

SIMON

VEGETABLES GROWING INTO THE GROUND are more yang by nature and, if baked, the yang element is increased. If you want more yang, bake them for longer or add more salt. The syrup, wine and thyme counter the yang; add more of these if you want a balanced dish. The yang recipe is helpful for working through difficult times and overcoming challenges.

STEVEN

THE ROASTING PROCESS brings out the sweetness of the vegetables, giving them a lovely richness that complements their natural flavours. Rice syrup is a healthy and organic way to sweeten the dish, although you can also use honey if you prefer.

watercress salad with couscous, mint and yoghurt dressing with lime juice

FOR THE COUSCOUS

125 g couscous

½ tsp Japanese seven spice

½ tsp ground nutmeg

100 ml clear vegetable stock
(see page 150)

FOR THE SALAD

50 g yoghurt, strained

juice of 1 lime

1 tbsp finely chopped Japanese
shiso or fresh basil

1 tbsp finely chopped mint

2 handfuls watercress, washed

½ yellow chilli (scotch bonnet
or jalapeño), finely chopped

¼ cucumber, thinly sliced

sea salt and fresh white pepper

50 g pine kernels, toasted

1 Place the couscous in a heatproof bowl with the seven spice and nutmeg. Put the stock in a saucepan and bring to a boil, then pour the hot stock over the couscous and leave to stand for 10 minutes to allow the couscous to absorb the stock and the flavours of the spices. Then fluff with a fork and leave to cool completely.

2 Mix the yoghurt with the lime juice in a bowl. Then toss together the shiso or basil, mint, chopped chilli, cucumber, couscous and yoghurt. Add the watercress, taking care not to over-mix or the watercress will become soggy. Season with salt and white pepper to taste. Divide the mixture into 4 portions and place on to serving plates. Sprinkle with the toasted pine kernels and serve.

SIMON

CUCUMBER, LIME AND WATERCRESS, when combined with couscous – one of the most yin grains – make this a distinctly yin dish. Yoghurt is one of the most yin of all the dairy foods, and the very light cooking style also adds yin. This dish has a predominance of metal, water and tree elements. It would be ideal when you want to relax and calm yourself.

STEVEN

TRY TO KEEP THIS REFRESHING SALAD LIGHT AND SUMMERY; be careful not to overdress the salad with too much yoghurt. Couscous is great because it absorbs the full flavour of any liquid you care to put it in – in this case the spiced vegetable stock. If you add the watercress at the very end, you will save it from wilting.

red bean cassoulet with whole grain barley, red wine and garlic

200 g dried red kidney beans

100 g whole grain barley

2 tbsp sunflower oil

2 onions, peeled and sliced

4 cloves garlic, peeled and sliced

200 ml clear vegetable stock
    (see page 150)

200 ml red wine

1 tbsp plain flour

salt and freshly milled black pepper

6 spring onions, finely chopped

2 tbsp chopped coriander leaves

1 Place the dried beans and barley in a bowl, cover with cold water and leave to soak overnight.

2 Preheat the oven to 150ºC. Heat 1 tbsp of the oil in a heavy-based casserole over a medium heat. Add the onions and garlic and cook for 1–2 minutes, stirring well. Drain the beans and barley, add the vegetable stock and bring to the boil. Pour in the red wine and return to the boil. Then reduce the heat and simmer for 10 minutes.

3 While the cassoulet is simmering, heat the remaining oil (1 tbsp) in a small saucepan over a low heat. Sprinkle in the flour and stir well to make a thick paste. Add this to the cassoulet and stir in thoroughly, making sure the paste is evenly distributed; season to taste and cover with a lid. Transfer the casserole to the preheated oven and cook for 45 minutes.

4 Remove from the oven and allow to rest for a few minutes. Taste and adjust the seasoning if necessary. Serve immediately, sprinkled with the finely chopped spring onion and coriander leaves.

SIMON

GENERALLY STEWS WILL BE MORE YANG than all other dishes, with the exception of baked foods. In this stew, the yang ingredients are the onions, beans, whole barley, flour and salt. The chilli, coriander and wine add a touch of yin chi energy, balancing the dish slightly; use less of these ingredients to make it more yang. The texture and make up of this dish give it a strong water and metal chi energy.

THE FLAVOURS IN THIS SUPERB DISH are excellent – all red wine, herbs and rich stock. This cassoulet can also make a flavoursome main dish. If you are not vegetarian, you can add one or two sausages; chop them into chunks, sear in a frying pan and then add them with the beans. You also can add a chopped red chilli if you want a little more spiciness.

STEVEN

inspired me to create this refreshing dessert. The basil is an unusual choice of herb to use in a dessert – it is stimulating for the tastebuds. You could also decorate with a sprig of mint as shown here.

STEVEN

FRUIT PROVIDES A STRONG YIN ENERGY, especially when raw and mixed with wine and fruit juice. Chilling the dish instantly adds more yin. The quality of five element chi energy for this dish will be predominantly water. This dish is ideal if you feel emotionally tense, as it helps you to become more peaceful, calm and passive.

SIMON

summer fruits steeped in muscat, with fresh basil

FOR THE SAUCE
200 ml Muscat or other sweet wine
200 g strawberries, washed and hulled
200 g raspberries, washed
juice of 2 oranges and ½ lemon
1 stick of cinnamon (optional)

FOR THE FRUITS
1 small ripe melon, scooped into small balls
115 g strawberries, washed and hulled
115 g blackcurrants, washed
115 g raspberries, washed
55 g blueberries, washed

TO FINISH
150 ml Muscat
8 leaves of fresh basil, shredded
1 tbsp icing sugar (optional)
4 tbsp thick soya cream or double cream

1 For the sauce, place the Muscat, the strawberries, raspberries and citrus juice in a food processor and blend to a smooth purée. Pass through a fine sieve into a clean pan.

2 Add the cinnamon (if using) to the saucepan and bring the purée slowly to the boil. Now drop in the other fruits – the melon balls, strawberries, blackcurrants, raspberries and the blueberries – and remove the pan from the heat immediately. Transfer the mixture to a clean bowl and allow to cool completely, then chill in the refrigerator for 6–8 hours.

3 Place 4 serving bowls in the freezer to chill. To finish, stir most of the 150 ml of Muscat into the chilled fruits and the purée mixture, then spoon into the chilled bowls. Decorate with basil leaves, then trickle the remaining Muscat over each portion. Dust with icing sugar (if using) and add a spoonful of soya cream or double cream to serve.

saffron poached pears with maple syrup and chestnut dressing

FOR THE PEARS

juice of 1 orange and ½ lemon

500 ml water

500 ml sweet white wine or Muscat

2 vanilla pods

2 pieces star anise

2 sticks cinnamon

1 tsp saffron threads

4 William pears (not overripe), peeled

FOR THE DRESSING

250 ml fromage frais (low fat)

150 g sweetened chestnuts, chopped

1 tbsp maple syrup

1 Mix all the ingredients for the pears – except the pears themselves – together in a large saucepan and bring to the boil, then lower the pears gently into the pan. Reduce the heat to a gentle simmer and cook for 30 minutes, ensuring that the pears are fully submerged – place a small plate over them to hold them down if necessary. Then remove the pan from the heat and allow the contents to cool completely – this cooling will intensify the colour of the pears.

2 To make the dressing, gently fold the fromage frais into the chopped chestnuts, then carefully stir in the maple syrup. Chill in the refrigerator until ready to serve.

3 Remove the cooled pears from the pan. You can serve them whole, but if you want to slice them, core with a small, sharp knife and carefully slice each from the base upwards without cutting through the stalk – thus leaving the fruit in one piece with 6–7 slices. Place each pear in a serving bowl and fan out the slices if you have made them. Drizzle with some of the cooking liquor and add the dressing to serve.

SAFFRON, VANILLA AND STAR ANISE are the key ingredients of this delicate and stimulating dish, adding a subtle twist to the bouquet of flavours. You can use clotted cream instead of fromage frais in the dressing for a slightly richer dish.

STEVEN

COOKING FRUITS MAKES THEM MORE YANG, concentrating the taste and making them sweeter. If you want to make the dessert even more yang, reduce or eliminate the wine and the honey. This dish is excellent for a cold day; the sweetness of the fruits will help you to relax, while the yang preparation will help to maintain a warm glow and provide energy.

SIMON

quick and easy passion fruit soufflé

25 g butter

25 g white caster sugar

150 ml freshly squeezed orange juice

2 tsp cornflour mixed with 1 tsp water

6 large egg whites

1 tbsp golden caster sugar

12 ripe passion fruits, halved

1 Rub 4 ramekins, each 9 cm in diameter, with butter and dust with white caster sugar. Then put them in the refrigerator to chill the butter.

2 Preheat the oven to 180°C. Place the orange juice in a saucepan over a low heat and bring to a gentle simmer, then whisk in the cornflour mixture. Cook over a low heat until the sauce thickens to the consistency of custard, then remove from the heat. If it becomes too thick, stir in a little more juice. If it is too thin, mix a little more cornflour with water and stir it in a little at a time, checking the results as you go.

3 Whisk the egg whites until stiff peaks form, then add the sugar and whisk for another 30 seconds.

4 Add the seeds and juices from the halved passion fruits to the orange 'custard', then allow it to cool completely before gently folding in the beaten egg whites. Spoon this mixture into the prepared and chilled ramekins and bake in the preheated oven, on the centre shelf, for 10 minutes until they are golden brown. Remove them from the oven and serve immediately. Serve with a simple dusting of icing sugar or a good-quality ice cream or sorbet.

STEVEN

THIS IS A FAIL-PROOF SOUFFLÉ because when you spoon the whites into the dish they already have height so they don't need to rise much, just cook to a golden brown.

TROPICAL FRUITS, SUCH AS PASSION FRUITS AND ORANGES, are more yin than those grown in colder climates. Along with the sugar, they make this dessert much more yin. Rich and sweet, this dish is both stimulating and satisfying.

SIMON

STEVEN

AMERICAN PANCAKES can also be made into a savoury dish by eliminating the cinnamon and maple syrup and adding some chopped parsley, lemon juice and glazing them with goat's cheese.

THE WHEAT FLOUR AND EGG make this recipe a relatively yang dessert. The cooking process is also yang, adding more fire chi energy to the ingredients. Serve with extra syrup or raw fruit to make the pancakes more yin. This dessert is perfect if you feel the need for extra energy on a cold day.

SIMON

american pancakes with maple syrup

150 g plain flour, sifted

1 tsp baking powder

1 egg

175 ml milk

1 tbsp almond or grape seed oil

1 tsp cinnamon powder

150 ml pure maple syrup or to taste

1 Sift the flour and baking powder together in a bowl. In a separate bowl, whisk together the eggs and milk until creamy, then add the flour and baking powder mixture. Beat into a smooth batter, then press through a sieve into a clean bowl.

2 Heat the oil in a pancake or frying pan over a medium-high heat. Once it is hot, drain the excess oil into a small, heatproof jug to use for the pancakes you make next. Ladle a quarter of the batter into the pan – it should be roughly 1 cm thick. Cook until brown underneath, or until little perforations appear on the top surface. Then flip it over and cook on the other side for the same amount of time, or until equally brown and perforated.

3 Remove from the pan and set the pancake aside to keep warm while you cook the others by placing it on a preheated ovenproof plate in the oven at a low temperature.

4 Repeat 3 more times with the remaining batter. Serve each pancake whole, or cut each into 6 triangles and stack the triangles one on top of another; dust with cinnamon powder and smother in maple syrup.

apricot ice cubes

250 g dried apricots
500 ml water
1 tbsp lemon juice
4 sprigs mint
4 tbsp crème fraîche
(optional)

1 Place the dried apricots in a saucepan and cover with the water. Bring to the boil over a medium heat, then simmer for 10–15 minutes until the apricots are soft and tender.

2 Remove the pan from the heat and blend the contents in a food processor or liquidizer. Stir in the lemon juice, then pour the apricot mixture into 4 ice cube trays. (I use round ice cubes to give a more classical appearance, but you can also use other shapes, such as stars or hearts, depending on the mood of your meal.) Freeze for a minimum of 3 hours.

3 To serve, simply dip the ice cube trays into warm water for 10 seconds and turn out the frozen cubes. Pile them into tall glasses, garnish each with a sprig of mint and serve. If you want a more satisfying dessert, spoon a dollop of crème fraîche onto each portion or serve with a small dish of it so that your guests can help themselves. For a more stylish effect, you can mix the cubes with purple cubes made in the same way from prunes.

THIS MAKES THE PERFECT DESSERT AFTER A LARGE MEAL. It is refreshingly stimulating and leaves you wanting more. It's such a wonderfully simple idea; take some tasty and plump dried fruit, purée it and make it into a kind of sweet sorbet. Try the same recipe with a variety of different dried fruits, such as prunes or plump sultanas. You can keep the ice cubes in their trays in the freezer for up to a month, so make it in bulk if you entertain frequently.

STEVEN

THE APRICOTS AND LEMON JUICE are relatively yin ingredients, and the freezing process adds more yin water chi energy. The dessert will be effective at taking heat out of the body, helping you to feel light and fresh on a hot day. The strong yin quality means it would not be appropriate in cold weather or when you are very low in energy. This dessert can be associated strongly with the five element water. Best for a burst of refreshment, this desert is great for freshening yourself for a hot afternoon or evening, especially if you want to feel light and cool.

SIMON

roasted peaches with brazil nut and date stuffing

FOR THE PEACHES

50 g shelled brazil nuts

100 g stoned fresh or dried dates

½ tbsp sweet almond or grape seed oil

4 large white peaches, peeled, halved and stoned
    (not overripe)

150 ml sweet white wine

25 ml brandy

75 ml fresh orange juice

FOR THE CHAMPAGNE GLAZE

4 medium egg yolks

1 tbsp honey

60 ml champagne or sparkling wine

1 Preheat the oven to 200°C. Roast the nuts in the oven for 10 minutes. Meanwhile, make the champagne glaze. Fill a saucepan half-full with water, so you can sit a bowl on the rim without the base of the bowl touching the water. Bring the water to a boil, then reduce the heat to simmer. Place the yolks in the bowl and whisk in ½ tbsp of the boiling water. Now add the honey and whisk the mixture over the simmering water until light and fluffy and twice the original volume. Now drizzle the champagne in slowly, whisking it in, then set aside.

2 Remove the brazil nuts from the oven (do not switch off the oven) and rub them inside a tea towel to remove the skins. Now blend the nuts and dates together in a food processor.

3 Heat the oil in an ovenproof frying pan over high heat and place the peaches, cut-side down, in the pan. Cook the cut sides for 1 minute until they are brown, then turn. Pour in the wine, brandy and orange juice. Transfer to the preheated oven for 10 minutes until the peaches are tender. Meanwhile, preheat the grill to a high setting. Remove the pan from the oven and spoon the nut and date mixture into the hollow left by the stone. Pour over the champagne glaze and grill until golden.

A REALLY FLAVOURSOME DESSERT, this peach dish provides an excellent way to impress dinner guests. Although they are lovely on their own, I like to serve them with a hearty dollop of clotted cream. The healthier chef may prefer to use low-fat crème fraîche or fromage frais. I always use a confectionery blowtorch to get that perfect finish on the glaze, but a grill will work just fine.

STEVEN

ALTHOUGH THE PEACHES, DATES, WINE AND BRANDY are all more yin, the baking process adds fire chi energy to make this recipe more yang. The sweetness of the fruit creates more soil chi energy. This is real comfort food – the finished dish creates a warm, relaxed, satisfied feeling in your abdomen, perfect for a winter evening meal in front of a roaring open fire.

SIMON

menus for success 3

A great meal depends on more than just delicious food: you also need to create the right ambience for the occasion. This chapter explains how you can plan your menu, prepare and cook the ingredients, present the finished dishes and decorate your table and dining area to positively influence the mood and behaviour of your guests and yourself. So, whether you're planning a romantic dinner for two, a harmonious family lunch or a formal celebration meal, make sure the energy of the food and the atmosphere are ideal for success.

feng shui and your dining area

IN THIS CHAPTER we show you how to choose the right menu and create the ideal atmosphere for nine different occasions, ranging from a satisfying meal for kids to a passionate dinner for two.

Chi is the all-important ingredient of any meal, so before you start choosing your recipes and writing out a shopping list, you first have to consider the kind of chi you should be promoting. When planning a quiet evening in, for example, you need to encourage a calming yin energy in both the food you prepare and the atmosphere in which you eat it; to stimulate conversation and laughter at a lively dinner party, on the other hand, you should create a more yang ambience. The five elements should also be considered (see pages 16–19). The pages that follow set out guidelines for matching chi to nine different food-related situations; once you have understood these basic principles, you will be able to plan and cater for all sorts of occasions with equal success.

There are many things you can do to ensure that you achieve the right type of chi. First, you should carefully choose the type of food you serve, as it will influence the chi of those who eat it. Throughout the chapter you will find mouth-watering recipes that not only look and taste wonderful but also have a range of different effects on your chi. Second, you can slow or speed the chi according to the colours, materials and textures of the crockery, cutlery, glassware and table linen you use. Third, the way in which you set and accessorise your table and decorate your dining area will subtly influence your mood and that of your guests. And fourth, think carefully about your seating plan, as the direction you face when you eat will have a tremendous impact on how you respond to the food, the atmosphere and to those around you.

The pages that follow are packed with suggestions for how to arrange your dining area with the appropriate type of chi in mind, varying from simple tips on the best colour for candles, for example, to more complicated considerations, such as the ideal table shape. There's no need to follow all of these recommendations: just choose those that suit you and your home. You certainly don't need to change the tables and chairs every time you entertain!

INFLUENCING CHI WITH COLOUR

Colour is of prime importance to Feng Shui eating as it is a very effective but inexpensive way to create a mood. You can use colour on a variety of different levels. Specific shades can be used to make you feel more yin or more yang; red and orange, for example, are more yang hues, while pale blue and green are more yin (see pages 10–15). Colours can also be used to strengthen, nourish or calm the prevailing five element energies (see pages 16–19), bringing a more specific feeling to the room, or to present a contrast with the food itself – a bright green salad served on a pale yellow plate or a delicate risotto in a bold blue bowl, for example. Of course, it would be impractical to repaint your dining room each time you want a change of atmosphere, but it is easy to introduce colour to the table in the form of tablecloths, napkins, flowers and other

THE DINING AREA AND EACH PERSON'S POSITION AT THE TABLE PLAY A KEY ROLE IN THE SUCCESS OF YOUR MEAL.

FACING NORTH

HELPFUL FOR feeling
introspective and calm
DANGERS being uncommunicative

FACING NORTH-WEST

HELPFUL FOR
dignity and wisdom
DANGERS becoming too
serious and self-righteous

FACING NORTH-EAST

HELPFUL FOR being humourous
and entertaining
DANGERS being thoughtless
and unsympathetic

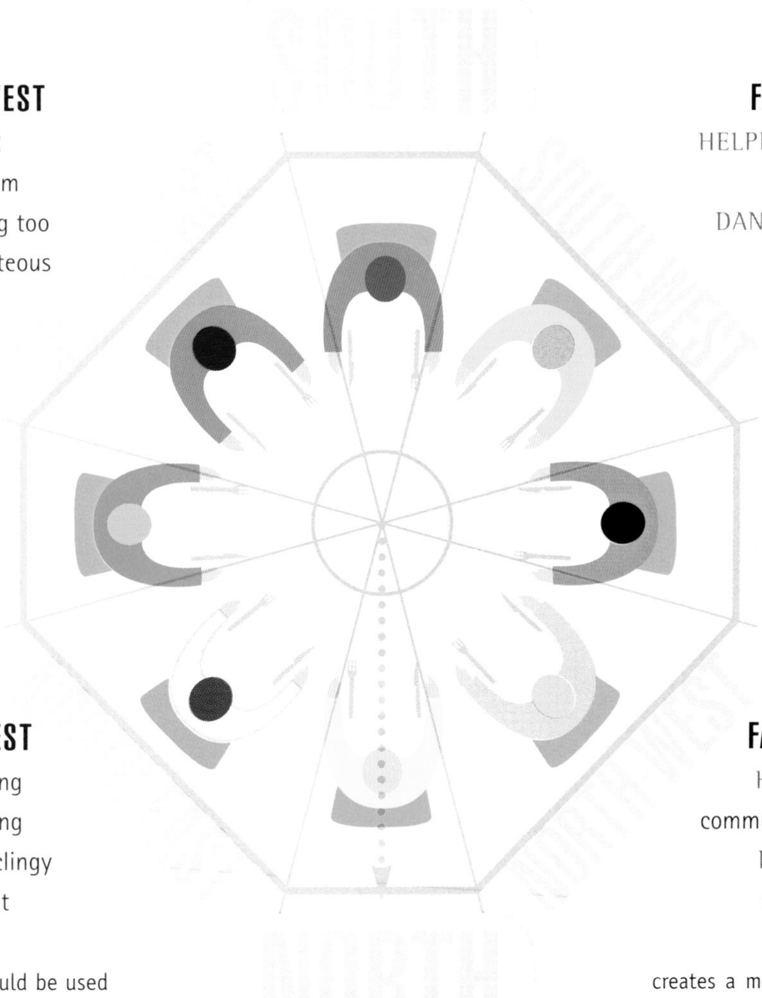

FACING WEST

HELPFUL FOR
pleasure and fun
DANGERS becoming
over-indulgent

FACING EAST

HELPFUL FOR self-
confidence and enthusiasm
DANGERS becoming
impatient

FACING SOUTH-WEST

HELPFUL FOR being
considerate and caring
DANGERS becoming clingy
and over-dependent

FACING SOUTH-EAST

HELPFUL FOR being
communicative and open-minded
DANGERS becoming
dreamy and sensitive

FACING SOUTH

HELPFUL FOR expression and
excitement
DANGERS becoming proud
and over-emotional

accessories. Bright shades should be used during the day while darker shades of the same colour work best in the evening. Different shades of a colour can be used to produce subtle changes in the chi energy. Pastels, for example, are always more yin and softer than the full-strength colours. The larger the area of any colour, the greater its influence will be. Strong colours like red and black will be effective even when they cover a relatively small surface area; often just a touch of a colour – a napkin or the cutlery – will be sufficient. Cream is associated with healing, health, peacefulness and well-being, while white creates a more competitive, motivational and sharper atmosphere. Yellow tones evoke comfort and warmth and represent nourishment and sustenance, good for keeping conversation on an even keel. Blue has soothing qualities, reducing tension and stress, but can also have an inspiring or exhilarating effect. Red is the colour of good fortune, happiness and romance. If you want to create a more passionate, expressive atmosphere, add small amounts of bright purple. Green is the colour of new life, supplying a fresh and uplifting ambience for a relaxed but stimulating environment.

establish an air of **formality**

MAJOR CELEBRATIONS, SUCH AS AN ANNIVERSARY OR ENTERTAINING IMPORTANT CLIENTS FOR THE FIRST TIME, DEMAND AN AIR OF FORMALITY TO CREATE THE PERFECT ENVIRONMENT. THEY ARE INVARIABLY DIGNIFIED SITUATIONS, REQUIRING THE YANG CHARACTERISTICS OF CEREMONY AND DECORUM, WHICH ARE ASSOCIATED WITH METAL CHI ENERGY.

A formal event brings out high standards of etiquette, manners and dress, and results in a heightened yang feeling. This encourages people to interact with awareness and dignity.

MENU PLANNING

A meal served in a formal setting demands a lengthy period of time in which to be served and eaten it. The atmosphere should be conducive to polite conversation or business matters, and you should allow long breaks between courses. You may be seated for several hours, especially if you finish the meal with coffee, liqueurs and speeches.

Rich yang foods would be appropriate for such an occasion as the guests are not expected to do anything after eating and need to feel satisfied. Steven's first course, the tempura of tuna, is distinctly rich, and draws on the traditions and history of Japan for its inspiration. The tempura batter should be light and crisp, making the whole dish satisfying without being filling and spoiling the guests' appetites. The tuna makes this a more yang starter while the tempura preparation adds more tree and fire chi energy, invigorating the guests and providing positive, sparkling chi to promote sociability.

The soufflé of sole with salmon and horseradish mousseline is another classic dish – this time European. It is a refined choice, in keeping with the formal theme. The sole and salmon make this a more yang dish, although the cooking style is more yin with more tree chi energy, good for new discussions and revitalising the spirit.

An old wine that has some history to it, such as a grand cru white burgundy, is the ideal beverage. If appropriate, finish the meal with an older port.

YOUR SURROUNDINGS

The best colours for formal occasions are maroon, silver, gold, red, off-white and light grey. A splash of rich maroon or red can be used to provide a dominant yang atmosphere and maintain a ceremonious tone. Silver adds metal chi energy, encouraging respect and dignity. Gold creates a more opulent chi energy, although too much can be ostentatious. Pale grey, cream and off-white can be used as background colours, giving a dignified, authoritative ambience.

Metal or silver-painted objects or ornaments will bring metal chi into the room. Antique silver photograph frames are perfect. Round or square metal-framed mirrors can be used to enhance the sense of ceremony and structure in the room. Wavy or uneven shapes will weaken metal chi energy.

One feature that will increase metal chi energy and add structure is a pendulum clock. Ideally the clock will have as many metal parts as possible and make an audible ticking. The sound and movement of the pendulum add rhythm to the surroundings.

If the meal is in the evening, consider dining by candlelight to create a more exciting atmosphere. If you prefer to use artificial light, position bulbs high in the room so that their light reflects up off the walls or ceiling to avoid direct glare. This provides a more subtle, calming atmosphere. Some bulbs or lightshades have their own integral reflector, which creates a soft, ambient lighting.

SEATING PLAN

The more formal directions to face are north-west, south, south-west and west, the directions holding social and organising influences. However, you may want to consider the directions in

a formal
menu

SPICED TUNA TEMPURA
WITH MIRIN
DRESSING

STEAMED SOLE
WITH SALMON AND
HORSERADISH
MOUSSELINE

CHOCOLATE AND
PINEAPPLE RAVIOLI
WITH PISTACHIO
PARFAIT AND MANGO
COULIS

serves 4

terms of suiting your guests' characters. A shy person may benefit from facing south-east, south or south-west – sunny directions that help people feel outgoing, expressive and friendly. Conversely, an excitable and overbearing person may be best placed facing north, which exerts a calming influence. Find the effects of the eight directions on page 67.

Powerful positions include those facing the door or the longest part of the room, in full view of the proceedings.

ADD EXTRA OPULENCE TO YOUR MEAL WITH A SILVER COFFEE SERVER, PREFERABLY ANTIQUE. THIS ADDS A PRISTINE END TO THE MEAL, REMINDING YOUR GUESTS OF THE FORMALITY OF THE OCCASION.

table setting

A LARGE, DARK-WOOD TABLE would be perfect for this occasion, adding an air of dignity and tradition. If you do not have a dark-wood table, use a white linen tablecloth. An oval shape is most appropriate, but use a rectangular table if you want to give the people sitting at each end of the table greater prominence. A round table is the next best choice. If you only have a square table, place a long centrepiece down its centre to give the impression of length.

When setting the table, use a maroon-coloured tablecloth to give the impression of opulence, or a white one if you prefer a simpler, sleeker appearance. Silver cutlery, napkin holders and candlesticks will bring more north-western energy to the setting, which will further encourage a sense of ceremony. As a centrepiece, choose a large, impressive flower arrangement with a mixture of blooms and greenery.

White and red flowers, especially roses or carnations, are ideal for a formal occasion. The arrangement should be set in a vase or planter of silver or gold that reinforces the impression of formality. Alternatively, use a china vase that has a regal pattern with a traditional theme or an antique quality about it.

ANTIQUES One way to create a formal environment is to bring older or grander-looking objects into the dining room. Items made of solid, dark wood or furniture upholstered in deep maroons are particularly suitable. Alternatively, introduce an element of the past to suggest a sense of long-standing tradition. A sculpture or picture of an historic event, or an old, posed photograph can help to establish an atmosphere of solidity.

SEA SALT Try placing a small dish of sea salt on the floor or a low shelf to purify and refresh the chi energy of the room. Place dishes in the north-east and south-west to stabilise the ebb and flow of soil energy.

tempura of tuna with mirin dressing

FOR THE SHOYU AND MIRIN DRESSING

100 ml shoyu sauce

100 ml mirin

1 tbsp toasted sesame seeds

FOR THE TEMPURA BATTER

3 egg whites

juice of 1 lime

150 g cornflour, sifted

salt and freshly milled black pepper

FOR THE TUNA TEMPURA

1 tbsp cinnamon

1 tbsp allspice

1 tbsp coriander seeds

1 tbsp ground ginger

salt and freshly milled black pepper

4 tuna steaks, sliced
   approximately 10 x 3 x 3 cm

vegetable oil for deep-frying

mizano leaves and baby ruby chard to
   garnish

1 First, prepare the dressing. Boil the shoyu sauce and mirin in a saucepan and reduce until syrupy, about 5 minutes. Add the sesame seeds and leave to cool.

2 For the tempura, beat the egg whites until semi-stiff and fold in the lime juice. Whisk in the cornflour and add a little cold water until the batter is thickened to coating consistency. Season.

3 For the tuna, grind the spices together in a bowl and toss the tuna slices in them until they are completely coated. Store covered in clingfilm until needed.

4 In a deep-fat fryer, heat the oil to 175°C. Dip the tuna steaks in the batter and deep-fry for 10 minutes. Don't cook more than two steaks at a time because this will cause the temperature of the oil to drop.

5 Remove the tuna and cut on the bias, as shown below. Serve with the salad leaves and drizzle the shoyu and mirin dressing around the fish and the plate.

steven says

A FORMAL MEAL SHOULD BE CREATIVE and imaginative enough to show off your skills and enthusiasm, without fuss or mess. I have chosen the tempura followed by the sole dish and finally the ravioli because they arrive on the table in neat parcels – beautifully decorated and precisely cut – observing the ritual of ceremony. You will need to begin preparing the parfait the day before.

steamed sole with salmon and horseradish mousseline

150 g salmon fillet, skin removed

salt and freshly milled black pepper

1 egg white

150 ml double cream

1 tbsp grated fresh horseradish

1 tbsp chopped fresh chives

2 lemon soles (30 g each), skinned
     and filleted off the bone

FOR VEGETABLE LATTICE

1 courgette

1 large carrot, peeled

a knob of butter

200 ml lobster bisque (see page 151)

1 Butter and refrigerate 4 rings or round cutters (8 cm across and 4 cm deep). Blend the salmon in a food processor, add the seasoning, egg white, double cream, horseradish and chives and blend again. Cover and chill.

2 Season the sole fillets well and use half of each filleted sole to line each ring or cutter. (I frequently line the buttered rings or cutters with strips of lightly blanched leeks to give a little extra colour and texture, see above.) Place each ring on greaseproof paper and fill the centre of each ring with the salmon mousse.

3 Preheat the oven to 100°C. Place the rings in a fish steamer for approximately 7 minutes. Check that the fish is cooked; it should be opaque and feel tender when pressed.

4 Meanwhile, slice the courgette and carrot into thin strips (½ cm thick and 14 cm long), plunge into boiling water for 2 minutes and immediately refresh in cold water.

5 Use a spatula to lift each ring from the steamer. Peel off the grease-proof paper and gently remove each ring. Place the fish rounds on warmed plates and keep warm in low oven until ready to serve.

6 Lay the strips of courgette in rows, leaving a small gap between them, and then weave strips of carrot over and under the courgette at right angles. When latticed, use the cutters or rings to cut out four neat rounds. Place on a baking tray, brush with a little melted butter, season and then place in the oven for 5 minutes to warm through.

7 Warm the lobster bisque in a saucepan. Place one lattice on top of each fish round, pour the lobster bisque around the outside, and serve.

chocolate and pineapple ravioli with pistachio parfait and mango coulis

FOR THE PISTACHIO PARFAIT

6 egg yolks

150 ml water

250 g caster sugar

25 g pistachio nuts, chopped

2 tsp pistachio paste

225 ml double cream

FOR THE CHOCOLATE PASTA

50 g strong flour

25 g cocoa powder

2 egg yolks

1–2 drops water

FOR THE PINEAPPLE FILLING

1 ripe pineapple, peeled

100 ml Kahlua rum

2 vanilla pods

100 g brown sugar

1 egg white

250 ml stock syrup for cooking
    (see page 152)

FOR THE MANGO COULIS

1 mango

juice of 1 lemon

25 ml water

1 Prepare the parfait. Whisk the egg yolks in a blender until risen and frothy. Heat the water and sugar in a saucepan and boil for 3 minutes. Slowly pour the hot mixture into the yolks and blend until mixed and cooled. Add the pistachio nuts and paste and blend for a further minute.

2 Whip the double cream until it forms a ribbon-like trail when the whisks are lifted. Fold the double cream into the yolks and pour into 4 circular moulds, 5 cm deep and 10 cm in diameter. Freeze for 24 hours.

3 Place all the chocolate pasta ingredients into a liquidizer and blend well. Cover and rest for 1 hour.

4 Cut 4 slices from the pineapple, approximately 6 mm thick, cover them and put them to one side. Dice the rest of the pineapple and cook it in a hot pan with the rum, vanilla and sugar until it reduces to a jam, which will take about 20 minutes. Then, brown the 4 whole slices of pineapple under a very hot grill until they are caramelised. Leave them to cool.

5 Roll out the pasta dough to a 4 mm thickness on a floured board. Cut out 8 circles – 4 with a diameter of 10 cm, and 4 with a diameter of 16 cm. Place a spoonful of the pineapple jam on each of the smaller circles. Brush egg white around the rims of the smaller circles and press the larger circles on top, sealing well.

6 Heat the stock syrup over a medium heat until it is nearly boiling. Submerge the ravioli, 2 at a time, and cook for 1 minute. Remove, drain and place in the refrigerator to cool.

7 Prepare the coulis. Peel and stone the mango. Dice the flesh and blend it in a liquidizer with the lemon juice and water. Pass through a fine sieve. Set to one side and refrigerate.

Serve by removing a parfait from the moulds and placing each one onto a pineapple ring. Top this with a chocolate ravioli parcel and pour the mango coulis around the base. You can decorate your finished dish with sugar or wafer decorations or a sugar lattice or serve plain.

get in the mood for romance

INCREASE THE ROMANTIC ENERGY OF A DINNER FOR TWO WITH THE RIGHT BALANCE OF FOOD AND DECOR. THE AIM IS TO CREATE A COSY, RELAXED ATMOSPHERE IN WHICH YOU FEEL BOTH INTIMATE AND LOVING. THE PERFECT ROMANTIC DINNER DRAWS ENERGY FROM THE ELEMENTS OF BOTH SOIL, FOR COMFORT AND SECURITY, AND METAL, FOR ROMANCE AND PLEASURE.

Romance is about feeling intimate with someone and, ideally, bringing your chi energy fields together to merge in a harmonious way. Feelings of excitement, intrigue and sexual interest will encourage the process, as will empathy and a mutual understanding.

On one level, the proper setting can help you think more romantically, especially if you can easily imagine being in an intimate, loving situation with the other person. At the same time, deeper feelings of pleasure, lust or desire can give the situation a powerful charge of chi energy.

MENU PLANNING

One of the ways to feel more cosy and intimate with someone is to share food with him or her. Steven's nabe – an Eastern type of hot pot – is ideal; the foods are cooked together in the same liquid and you can share the dish, eating from the same bowl. Such a meal is better than foods cooked separately because their chi energy will not mix as strongly. Sharing and helping each other to eat will bring you closer together.

It is important not to eat a meal that is too heavy as it may cause you or your guest to feel overly tired. A meal that is rich and salty could be too yang, leaving you feeling practical rather than playful. Too yin a meal could leave you overly relaxed, without the motivation for romance.

Shellfish and other seafood, especially oysters, have a chi energy that is associated with sex and would therefore be helpful to increase feelings of sexual desire between you.

A sugary dessert, such as ice cream, will give you a temporary rush of energy at the end of your meal and, when combined with chocolate, can act as an aphrodisiac. This can balance the more yang seafoods in the starter and main course. Similarly, stimulating drinks would help to make a more interesting meal. Try mixing a cocktail before you eat. A lighter, more fruity red wine would be best with the meal. Don't serve too many cold or iced drinks as this increases yin energy and may dampen your romantic fervour. Coffee at the end of the meal can act as a stimulant and keep you both alert. A black coffee would be more effective than one with milk.

Soil and metal tastes are helpful for romance, increasing comfort and pleasure respectively. These can be found in Steven's use of honey, rice syrup and ginger.

YOUR SURROUNDINGS

The main colours of romance are cream, red and pink. According to the principles of Feng Shui, cream is associated with being sexual. It also can make a relaxing, sensual background colour and would be an appropriate shade for a tablecloth. Red adds style and romance, so be sure to add a touch of red in the form of napkins, candles, flowers or other decorative details. Pink is associated with pleasure, and accessories in this colour would help to bring out the playful intrigue of romance.

Red or pink roses create the best chi energy for a romantic meal. A pair of long-stemmed red roses in a tall, slender vase in the centre of the table embodies the mood of romance and symbolically reinforces the idea of intimacy and togetherness.

Soft, drawn curtains in pinks and creams add a luxurious, opulent feeling which can help to boost relaxation, intimacy and confidence. Silk and brocade used abundantly provide the best chi energy for romance.

Decorate your room with pairs of things, such as two candles, or an ornament or picture of a pair of people or animals. Alternatively, find objects that you can group in pairs – match up two plants or move two pictures together, for example. When choosing a sculpture, find one representing a couple. Try to avoid solitary figures or single images.

SEATING PLAN

The best position to face is west, the direction of the setting sun. This exposes you to chi energy associated with sunset, the evening and the pleasures of life. Alternatively, face north to align yourself with the chi energy of the night and sex. This more affectionate and intimate chi energy can help you to feel closer to your partner. If you face south, the chi energy associated with passion, self-expression and emotion can help if you want to increase your passion (see pages 98–103) for each other.

Choose whichever of these directions would be best for you and your romantic partner. If, for example, you tend to be shy and want to be more expressive, sit facing south. Conversely, if you tend to be too serious, you can promote playfulness by facing west. North is ideal if you tend to monopolise situations or risk overpowering your partner. It is possible that your room may only suit sitting facing certain directions. If this is the case, choose the best of those available for you and your partner. Other helpful directions for the romantic setting include facing south-east and south-west.

Try different seating arrangements at different stages of your romantic evening. Sit facing each other while you eat to make you more aware of each other and increase eye contact. If you sit at right angles to each other, you will feel closer and this will encourage more physical contact. Sitting next to each other enhances intimacy and understanding, and you may want to move into this position for dessert.

romantic menu

KING PRAWN TEMPURA WITH
SPICY SHOYU DIPPING SAUCE

ORIENTAL NABE (HOT POT)

GREEN TEA ICE CREAM
WITH CHOCOLATE SAUCE

serves 2

table setting

ALTHOUGH THE DINING ROOM can be kept simple and relaxing, it is best to have a table setting that adds sparkle and energy and induces pleasure, fun and excitement.

Shiny metal cutlery also speeds the movement of chi. The reflective surface of the metal disperses chi in different directions, keeping the energy active and moving. The same would apply to metal napkin holders, candlesticks or other decorative items. Ideal metals would be silver or gold – silver is more formal, gold more opulent. If you prefer to use chopsticks to eat the nabe, use decorative ones in pink, red or purple.

Use tablecloths, napkins and crockery to slow the chi energy and soften the atmosphere, especially with the colours cream, pink, pale green and pastel blue.

PAIRING UP Pictures of couples or romantic subjects enhance the feeling of togetherness.

SOFT LIGHTING Rather than using direct lights and glaring lightbulbs, try uplighters which can be reflected off a wall or ceiling, although tablelighting that is lower creates a more cosy atmosphere and is more flattering on the human skin.

king prawn tempura with spicy shoyu dipping sauce

IDEAL CHAIRS Use comfortable, upholstered chairs in cream or pink. Alternatively, place soft fabrics or cushions in these colours on each chair.

6 prawns (3 each), king or tiger

1 tsp ground Chinese five spice

1 tsp ground ginger

1 tsp sea salt

1 tsp crushed black pepper

FOR THE TEMPURA BATTER

2 egg whites

juice of 1 lemon

a pinch of salt

100 g cornflour

vegetable oil for frying

FOR THE DIPPING SAUCE

100 ml of light shoyu sauce

1 tbsp honey

1 tbsp toasted sesame seeds

25 ml rice wine

1 red chilli, deseeded and chopped

TO GARNISH

a few rocket leaves, dressed with olive oil, lime juice and salt

1 If the prawns are uncooked, blanch them in simmering water (with a little olive oil and seasoning) or fish stock for 2 minutes and immediately refresh under cold or iced water. Pat dry using a sheet of kitchen paper.

2 Remove the shell from each prawn, leaving the tail intact. Mix the spices and ground ginger in a bowl with the salt and pepper. Toss the prawns in the spices until each is well coated.

3 Prepare the tempura. Whisk the egg whites with the lemon juice and salt until they peak. Then, whisk in the cornflour until the mixture is thicker (but still fluffy). If necessary, add cold water to make it thinner, or more cornflour to thicken it.

4 To make the dipping sauce, heat the shoyu sauce with the honey, add the sesame seeds and wine. Cook until the sauce thickens, add the chilli, pour into a dish and chill.

5 Heat the oil in a deep-fat fryer to 375°C. Holding the tails, dip the prawns into the batter and then drop them into the hot oil. Cook for exactly 1 minute then remove and drain. Serve hot with salad.

1. In a large saucepan, heat the oil over medium heat and gently cook the spring onions for 5 minutes until soft but not brown. Add the mushrooms and cook for a further 1–2 minutes.

2. Now add the vegetable stock, the red and green jalapenos, the daikon, the hoi sin sauce, the rice syrup, and the shoyu sauce. Simmer for 5 minutes, then taste. If it is too bitter, salty or sour, add a touch more hoi sin sauce and rice syrup. If it is too sweet add a little more shoyu sauce.

3. Add the noodles and juice from the oysters (strained through a fine sieve) and cook for a further 5 minutes.

4. Finally, add the oysters, chopped coriander and the cucumber. Simmer again for 5 minutes, then squeeze in the lime juice. Taste, season if necessary, and serve in the middle of the table in a large bowl.

oriental nabe (hot pot)
with rice noodles

1 tbsp grape seed oil

4 spring onions or shallots,
    cut in half

8 shiitake mushrooms, sliced

1 litre clear vegetable stock
    (see page 150)

2 red jalapeños, pickled
    (see page 149)

2 green jalapeños, pickled
    (see page 149)

1 small daikon, thinly shredded and
    pickled (see page 149)

2 tbsp hoi sin sauce

1 tbsp rice syrup or honey

1 tbsp shoyu sauce

50 g rice noodles

12 oysters from the shell, with juices
    reserved and passed through a fine
    sieve (or alternative shellfish)

1 bunch fresh coriander, chopped

a few slices of cucumber, thinly
    sliced and quartered

juice of 1 lime

salt and freshly milled black pepper

steven says

THIS IS ABOUT SHARING, LOVING AND HAVING FUN with an existing or prospective romantic partner. When it comes to food, consider dishes you have to cook together, eat together, and eventually clear up together! Dishes like the Japanese nabe, or even a fondue, will make you feel cosy and close, and offer that opportunity to get intimate with each other while enjoying a delicious meal.

USE CRYSTAL GLASSES TO ADD SPARKLE.
THESE WILL HELP THE AMBIENT CHI ENERGY
SPIN A LITTLE FASTER, REFLECTING OFF
THE HARD SHINY SURFACES.

If you're a vegetarian, you can use carrot, cauliflower, parsnip or mushrooms to replace the prawns in the starter. In the main course, the oysters are excellent aphrodisiacs, but you can also use any shellfish, including lobster, crawfish or crabs or mussels. Alternatively, use chunks of gently poached cod or hake. If you prefer a meatier version of the dish, try it with cooked chicken or with very thinly sliced raw beef cooked for 2 minutes on top of the nabe.

green tea ice cream with chocolate sauce

1 tbsp of fresh green tea leaves
250 ml double cream
6 egg yolks
150 g caster sugar
250 ml soya cream

FOR THE CHOCOLATE SAUCE

50 g plain dark or bitter chocolate
150 ml soya cream or milk
   or double cream

1 In a medium-sized saucepan, add the tea to the double cream and bring to the boil over high heat. Meanwhile, in a bowl, whisk together the egg yolks and sugar until they are pale and lemon-coloured. Add the warm double cream and tea mixture and whisk vigorously.

2 Now add the soya cream and whisk it in. Pour the mixture into an ice cream maker and churn until frozen. Alternatively, pour the mixture into a chilled bowl and freeze for 1 hour. After 1 hour, whisk thoroughly and freeze again for another hour. Now stir the mixture and freeze again until you are ready to serve – at least 1 hour.

3 Just before serving, melt the chocolate in a bowl set on top of a saucepan of boiling water. Whisk in the soya cream. Place the ice cream in serving bowls and accompany with the warm chocolate sauce.

THE KEY TO RELAXATION IS TO INCREASE
YOUR YIN ENERGY, CALMING STRESS AND
EASING THE PRESSURE OF DAY-TO-DAY
PROBLEMS. SURROUND YOURSELF WITH
TRANQUIL WATER ENERGY — THE
ELEMENT FOR DEEP CONTEMPLATION
AND CALM — WITH FLOWING SHAPES
OR CREAM COLOURS.

the perfect recipe for relaxation

It is essential for our health and happiness to take time to unwind properly from the daily stresses of life. Most commonly we relax when we sleep, however, sometimes a night's sleep is not enough and we need to take further steps to relax. Stretching, meditation and walking in natural surroundings all can help achieve this. In addition, the food you eat and how you eat it will affect your ability to relax, and a quiet meal can be the perfect way to rebalance your system.

MENU PLANNING

When you're stressed, you may find that your body secretes more acids into your stomach. Some of these are absorbed into the bloodstream, and some remain in the stomach and intestine where they can cause a number of digestive problems. You should therefore try to reduce acidity in your diet if you are feeling stressed and need to relax. You should also reduce salt as it can make it harder for your body to cope with stress, particularly your heart and arteries which tighten in times of stress. This highly yang ingredient can make you feel the adverse effects of stress more acutely and should be minimised.

In general, meals with a creamier texture and a sweeter taste make you feel better able to relax. These types of food have a relatively settled soil energy, bringing comfort and feelings of security. Lightly cooked yin foods, such as blanched vegetables, will also help you cope with stress.

Steven's menu for relaxation starts with a flavoursome, but light, soup. The vegetable ingredients help to create a soothing yin dish. Use clear vegetable stock instead of dry white wine if you want to reduce acidity. In general, soup will have a flowing water chi energy, making it easier to release tension.

The main dish is a braised vegetable mornay, bringing together the natural sweetness of the braised parsnips, carrots and onions to make this a lovely sweet, yin dish. The rice syrup increases the yin sweetness further. Again, replace the wine with vegetable stock to reduce acidity. Couscous makes the perfect accompaniment; it is a light, yin grain that enhances calm.

The honey and raspberry fool with cointreau and raisins makes a tasty yin dessert. The yoghurt adds creamy richness, while the honey and raisins are natural sweeteners. This dish will have predominantly soil energy, bringing comfort and support.

A warm, soothing drink will help you to relax. Avoid acidic and stimulating drinks, such as coffee or soft drinks with added sugar. Try organic apple juice warmed up or mixed with boiling water, or teas that don't have caffeine, such as camomile. Japanese bancha twig tea is helpful at the end of a meal as it is slightly alkaline, helping to reduce acidity.

Try to relax while eating. Feeling tense encourages you to secrete more acids into stomach increasing the risk of over acidity, which can cause discomfort and digestive troubles. Always sit down so that your stomach adopts the ideal shape for digestion. Try to leave a space between your main course and dessert because some of the ingredients in your dessert will be quicker to digest than those in a typical main course, leading to bloating, flatulence and discomfort. When eating, try to chew your foods at least thirty times so that your food breaks down and mixes properly with your saliva. This will make your food less acidic and easier to digest.

YOUR SURROUNDINGS

In order to relax, you need to find ways to make your own chi energy more yin. Yin energy slows down the active, impatient side of your nature and enables your contemplative and peaceful feelings to dominate. A yin diet coupled with a yin environment are the best ways to help you to unwind and find greater peace in your life.

Use yin colours, particularly cream, pale blue, pale green and pink. The more pale or light the hue of any colour, the more yin and relaxing.

You also need to slow down the flow of chi energy and, in particular, avoid places or situations where chi energy flows along a straight line and picks up speed. This is most likely to happen along corridors, around the edge of sharp protruding corners, and wherever you have several doors in a straight line. The easiest way to make a space more relaxing around these features is to use plants, strategically placed in front of corners and along straight passageways, to radiate a natural chi energy and slow fast-flowing chi energy. A greater use of fabrics slows the flow of chi energy, so consider adding more curtains, rugs, carpets and cushions to the room.

Low, indirect lighting is most effective for a relaxing environment. Table lights placed on low surfaces are better because the light is not at an obtrusive level. Use a shade or direct the light onto a wall to avoid the direct glare of the bulb. Incandescent lights give off a slightly orange glow which can further increase the relaxing feel of the room.

Mirrors make the room yang and should be avoided if possible. If you have a large mirror, particularly if directly near the dining table take it down for the evening or drape a pastel-coloured cloth or curtain over it.

A collection of pale-coloured flowers is visually calming, particularly if the flowers have softer, less pointed shapes, such as lily-of-the-valley and iris. Place the flowers in a glass or opaque container with a curved shape.

Plants with rounded leaves generate soft, yin energy, with the result that they make a room feel peaceful and tranquil. Bushy plants help the whole room feel softer and relax the eyes and the mind. A ficus is the ideal example, along with cheese plants, money plants or rubber plants. Plants in general are particularly effective at cleansing the air and reducing noise in a room which will perfect an environment for relaxation.

Relaxing works of art, such as a countryside landscape in a watercolour finish, can help you to relax. Many people find scenes that include calm water relaxing, for example a picture of a lake or a slow-running river or stream. Any painting in muted colours and with flowing shapes

relaxing menu

CREAMY CELERIAC SOUP
WITH NUTMEG AND
CINNAMON

BRAISED VEGETABLE
MORNAY WITH
MUSHROOMS AND
SPINACH

HONEY AND RASPBERRY
FOOL WITH COINTREAU
RAISINS

serves 4

provides a calming ambience. If you want to decorate your dining room with a sculpture or ornament, choose one with flowing, soft shapes and gentle curves. These are associated with water chi energy, the most obvious example being a sculpture of the human body, especially when in a relaxed pose. Alternatively, choose another calming image, such as a sleeping animal.

Music can be an excellent way to alter your own chi energy. Sounds generate waves through the air, passing through your outer chi energy field. These waves can either stimulate or soothe this more superficial chi energy, effectively changing your mood and emotional state. Any music that does not have an obvious rhythm or repetitive beat is more yin and therefore more relaxing. Soft classical music would be a good example of relaxing music, but be aware – some pieces have very stirring movements and may suddenly change the mood.

The sound of water trickling over stones or of a waterfall is considered particularly relaxing in Feng Shui. This is because it covers the full range of tones and therefore helps to cover up any ambient sounds and fills the mind completely with its own rhythms.

You may find that you have unwittingly built up an emotional association between a particular sound or type of sound and a relaxing time in your life. A song from your summer holiday, for example, may remind you of relaxing on a warm golden beach or looking over beautiful scenery. Recalling or playing this song may make it easier for you to revive the same emotions of calm and relaxed tranquillity.

SEATING PLAN

When attempting to relax, try sitting so that you face one of the directions that relate to the setting sun or the night – north, north-west, west or south-west. Of these, the north has the most peaceful chi energy.

table setting

IDEALLY, A LESS CONVENTIONAL SHAPE, such as a kidney-shaped table or a table made up of a number of gentle curves, is preferable for increasing water energy. Otherwise, a round or oval table or one with rounded corners will promote yin energy. If you only have a sharp-cornered table, smooth the edges and corners by using a thick tablecloth.

Use low and comfortable chairs if you have them. Upholstered chairs encourage chi energy to move slowly, making it easier to feel relaxed. If you don't have upholstered chairs, use soft cushions or drape a cloth over the back of each one – a pale-coloured napkin, cushion cover or even a pillowcase would be ideal.

LAMPS Table lamps, wall-mounted lights and lights that shine through opaque glass, perforated material or coloured fabric, produce a warm, relaxing energy.

For all tables, a soft fabric tablecloth helps reduce the flow of chi energy. Choose one in a calm, relaxing yin colour, such as cream, pale blue or pale green.

Choose crockery, cutlery and tableware in yin colours and with curved water shapes and patterns to enhance the relaxing qualities of your meal. Wooden chopsticks or spoons, plates, napkin holders and candleholders provide the best kind of yin energy for comfort and relaxation.

Draw any curtains and cover the floors with mats and rugs. Soft patterns, such as a waves, a mottled effect or soft, irregular shapes, create a peaceful image.

CRYSTALS These scatter chi energy into of the room, helping the energy to reach into dark corners. Hang a single crystal by the window to bring sunlight into a dark room.

WATER FEATURES Water creates a relaxing, reflective atmosphere, especially when it trickles slowly, as it masks background noise. Feng Shui also makes great use of an aquarium, where both the water and the movement of the fish promote calm.

steven says

WHEN I THINK OF
RELAXING FOOD, I
dream of warm comforting
soup and a vegetable or fish
bake. I used to eat this sort
of food when I first went
into catering. I would come
home exhausted at about
midnight and my mother
would have left me some
soup, bread and a cheesy
bake. I would sit in front of
the television with my feet
up and a glass of wine in
my hand – and I was only
16 – nothing changes!

creamy celeriac soup with nutmeg and cinnamon

1 whole celeriac, peeled and diced into
　2 cm pieces
1 large onion, peeled and sliced
2 cloves garlic, peeled and sliced
500 ml double cream
250 ml clear vegetable stock
　(see page 150)
salt and freshly milled white pepper
freshly ground cinnamon and nutmeg

1 Place the celeriac, onion, garlic and cream into a saucepan over high heat and bring to the boil, stirring all the time. Add the stock and simmer until the celeriac is tender – approximately 15–20 minutes.

2 Purée the mixture in a food processor and pass through a fine sieve into the saucepan. Season to taste.

3 To serve, sprinkle with freshly ground cinnamon and nutmeg. If you drizzle 2 tablespoons of cold milk into each bowl of soup and whisk vigorously, you can obtain a good froth.

braised vegetable mornay with mushrooms and spinach

2 medium parsnips, peeled and cut
    into 8 cm strips

3 medium carrots, peeled and cut
    into 8 cm strips

2 medium onions, peeled and sliced

2 leeks, cut into 8 cm strips

1 tbsp rice syrup or honey

1 litre clear vegetable stock (see
    page 150) or 250 ml white
    wine and 750 ml water

1 sprig of thyme

2 cloves garlic, peeled and chopped

250 g field mushrooms, chopped

1 tbsp grape seed or light olive oil

1 tsp chopped fresh tarragon

salt and freshly milled black pepper

225 g baby spinach leaves

300 ml double cream

150 g freshly grated Parmesan cheese

2 large potatoes, peeled and sliced

1 Preheat the oven to 150°C. Place the parsnips, carrots, onions and leeks into a baking dish, add the rice syrup, stock, thyme and garlic. Season, cover with foil and braise for 45 minutes, then purée in a food processor until smooth.

2 Fry the mushrooms in a little oil over a medium-high heat for 1–2 minutes, add the tarragon and season. Add the raw spinach and stir in. Place the spinach and mushrooms around the base of the baking dish and then spread over the puréed vegetables.

3 Now prepare the cheese sauce. Bring the double cream to the boil in a saucepan over medium-high heat, whisking all the time. Then add 100 g of the grated Parmesan. Stir well and season to taste. Increase the oven temperature to 200°C.

4 Pour the cheese sauce over the vegetables in the baking dish and top with the sliced raw potatoes. Season well and bake for approximately 15 minutes. Remove the dish from oven, sprinkle the rest of the grated Parmesan cheese over the top and continue to cook until golden brown on top (approximately 5–10 minutes). Serve with a crisp green salad.

honey and raspberry fool with cointreau raisins

2 tbsp of dried raisins

2 tsp cointreau

2 tbsp of clear honey

400 g fresh raspberries

300 ml natural yoghurt

4 sprigs of fresh mint

1 Soak the raisins in the cointreau for 30 minutes. Add the honey and stir in, then add the raspberries and mix well, but gently so that the raspberries do not break up.

2 Transfer the mixture to a bowl and mix with the yoghurt. Chill until ready to serve.

3 When ready to serve, pour the mixture into chilled dessert glasses and top with a small sprig of fresh mint. Serve immediately.

BRING A FLOURISH OF CREATIVITY
TO YOUR HOME BY SPINNING THE
CHI ENERGY IN A DIFFERENT
DIRECTION, WHICH WILL ENABLE
YOU TO VIEW THE WORLD FROM
AN ENLIGHTENING NEW ANGLE.
SIT BACK AND SET YOUR
IMAGINATION FREE.

fresh food to inspire your creativity

Surrounding yourself with creative chi energy makes it easier for you to have original ideas and new insights, whether your interests are in art, music, writing, photography, film or theatre. Exposing yourself to the artistic works of others can help you to stimulate your own creative side.

A creative meal is one in which the food is mentally stimulating, generating inspired conversation and new ideas. The more extraordinary the experience, the more it will help to change your perception of a subject and develop creative ideas. A change of atmosphere or unfamiliar foods can give you a very different kind of chi energy that can stimulate your thought processes and encourage creative thinking.

Often it is great extremes of yin and yang energy that tend to produce more dynamic thinking, although it may be harder to put these ideas into practice. Each of the five elements can be creative in its own way – water can make you artistic, tree helps you to be productive, fire encourages self-expression, soil enables you to be more skillful and metal helps you develop stylishness. Incorporate each of these in your environment to promote an overall atmosphere of vitality and creativity.

MENU PLANNING

One of the ways to feel more creative is to have great variety in your foods. Sushi are an excellent way to achieve this because they provide a perfect opportunity to mix interesting ingredients. They can be made refreshing or provocative using Steven's recipes; the wasabi, used in the sushi or as a dipping sauce, is especially stimulating to the mind. The nori seaweed used to wrap the sushi is extremely high in minerals, supplying vital nutrients to the brain. Sushi are generally light and it is easy to feel satisfied without feeling full or heavy, which can severely affect your creative impulse.

Mixtures are more provoking, and a cocktail of different freshly squeezed fruit juices, for example, has the potential to change your chi energy quickly. More stimulating drinks would include lemon and ginger or peppermint tea, and black coffee.

YOUR SURROUNDINGS

The aim is to produce the kind of atmosphere in which you feel inspired to be creative. This is achieved by creating a bright, clean, open environment in which chi energy can move easily.

Stimulating, bright colours, such as red, yellow, purple, blue and green, are best for creativity. Use a neutral background shade, white or cream, for example, and highlight it with these bright, strong colours. Red is a dynamic yang colour that helps to increase activity and energy. Bright purple is strongly associated with passion and brings emotion into whatever you do. A strong yellow can help to activate the mind. A strong sky blue brings you greater vision and big ideas. Lively greens encourage you to feel more active, confident and progressive.

The most creative places are large and open, so set the table outside if you have a patio or garden and the weather is fine, or try to sit near or facing a window with a spacious view.

SEATING PLAN

The most creative direction to face at mealtimes is east, the direction of the sunrise. This exposes you to the chi energy associated with the beginning of the day and the spring time, which help you generate new ideas and get new projects off the ground. Facing south-east is also favourable as it helps to stimulate your imagination and is the best chi energy for being more artistic or finding new solutions. South is mentally stimulating and this fiery chi energy can help you to find powerful ways to express yourself. Alternatively, facing north aligns you with the chi energy associated with being independent and individual.

Choose whichever of these directions would be best for you. If you need to get started on a new project, for example, face east to get an extra burst of motivation and action. Conversely, if you feel that you have run out of new or interesting ideas, face south-east to enhance creative insight.

South would be best if you need help to get your creative ideas out in the open. North is ideal if you want to retreat inside yourself and come up with something original and different.

a creative menu

MARINATED TUNA SUSHI

SUSHI WITH MUSSEL
CEVICHE AND SESAME
SEEDS

BAKED TAMARILLO
WITH COCONUT AND
LEMONGRASS ICE

serves 4

BRIGHT LIGHTING INCREASES THE FLOW OF CHI ENERGY, PARTICULARLY IF IT IS DIRECTED UPWARD AND INTO CORNERS, EMPHASISING THE FEELING OF EXPLORING NEW SPACE. LOW-VOLTAGE HALOGEN LIGHTING IS INTENSE AND BRIGHT AND WOULD BE IDEAL, ALTHOUGH MANY TYPES OF HIGH-VOLTAGE LIGHT BULBS HAVE A SIMILAR EFFECT. COLOURED LIGHTING AND GLASS OR BRIGHT FABRIC SHADES CAN ALL BE USED TO MAKE A ROOM MORE STIMULATING.

table setting

A LARGE ROOM WITH A LARGE ROUND TABLE would be ideal for a creative atmosphere, the space giving an impression of extra room for mental expansion. Counter the effect of oval, square or oblong tables by positioning the place settings at uneven intervals. A shiny table surface, such as glass or a polished wood, provides a reflective energy excellent for creative thinking. Large glasses, plates and serving dishes with plenty of spare table space will all encourage you to expand your mind and ideas – an overcrowded table has a negative, restrictive effect. Shiny, metal cutlery encourages chi energy to move quickly, generating a mentally stimulating environment. Any unusual shapes can help to inspire new and innovative ideas.

INNOVATIVE TABLEWARE Use crockery with bright colours and patterns; swirling patterns bring more water energy to your meal, promoting reflection and deeper thought. Square-shaped plates and novel designs add a panache that can spark your imagination.

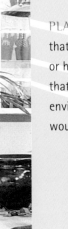

PLANTS AND FLOWERS Choose plants that grow upwards, rather than spreading or hanging, and those with pointed leaves that can help create a more lively environment. Palms, ferns and yuccas would all be good examples.

CANDLES A naked flame boosts fire chi, strongly associated with new ideas and quick thinking. Try placing candles in the southern part of the room; they will inflame the fire energy inherent in this part of the room and make a greater impact.

PAINTINGS AND SCULPTURES Choose provocative paintings or sculptures that make you think and stretch your imagination further. If you believe anything is possible, you are more likely to take on bigger challenges.

marinated tuna sushi

FOR THE MARINATED TUNA

2 tbsp sesame oil

1 tsp grated fresh ginger

1 tbsp shoyu sauce

juice of 2 limes

100 g tuna loin, cut into thin strips 4 x ½ x ½ cm

FOR THE SUSHI

5 tbsp Japanese or Thai glutinous rice

2 tsp salt

1 tbsp rice wine vinegar

1 tbsp granulated sugar

1 tsp wasabi paste

1 pkt nori seaweed (10 sheets)

100 ml shoyu sauce

wasabi paste to serve

1 Mix the marinade ingredients together and stir in the raw tuna. Cover and leave for 1–2 hours in the refrigerator.

2 Place the rice in a saucepan and cover with cold water. Bring to the boil. Add salt, cover and simmer until the rice has completely absorbed the water, usually 20 minutes. Remove from the heat and let stand, covered, for 10 minutes.

3 In another saucepan, bring the rice wine vinegar and sugar to the boil to dissolve the sugar. Then remove from the heat. Transfer the cooked rice into a clean non-metallic bowl. Pour in the vinegar/sugar mixture and gently fold into the rice to combine. Add the wasabi paste and stir it in well.

4 Using either a bamboo mat or clingfilm, place half a sheet of the seaweed on top and brush with a little shoyu sauce. Cover two-thirds of the seaweed with the rice mixture, leaving an empty strip running lengthways down one side. Place a line of tuna strips down the centre of the rice. Gently roll it up tightly, starting on the side covered with the rice – the nori should encase the rice and tuna, with some overlap to secure it in place. Repeat with the other sheets of seaweed. Slice each of the sushi rolls into 4–5 pieces, set on a serving dish and serve with shoyu sauce and wasabi.

sushi with mussel ceviche and sesame seeds

FOR THE MUSSEL CEVICHE

½ tbsp olive oil

2 shallots, peeled and finely chopped

2 cloves garlic, peeled and finely
    chopped

12 mussels, de-bearded and scrubbed

100 ml white wine vinegar

200 ml white wine

1 tbsp chopped dill

1 tbsp capers, chopped

black pepper

FOR THE SUSHI

5 tbsp Japanese or Thai
    glutinous rice

2 tsp salt

1 tbsp rice wine vinegar

1 tbsp granulated sugar

1 tsp wasabi paste

1 pkt nori seaweed
    (10 sheets)

2 tbsp toasted sesame seeds

100 ml shoyu sauce to serve

wasabi paste to serve

1 Prepare the mussel ceviche. Heat the oil in a saucepan over a low heat. Cook the shallots and garlic for 5 minutes until tender but not brown.

2 Increase the heat and add the mussels, the vinegar and the wine. Hold a lid down over the top and shake the pan vigorously to encourage the mussels to open. Cook for a further 3–5 minutes until the mussel shells have opened. Remove from heat and allow to cool.

3 Remove mussels from their shells and discard the shells. Put the meat back into the cooking juices, stir in the dill and capers and season with pepper. This can be kept refrigerated in a sealed container for up to a week – the flavours improve after 1–2 days.

4 Now cook the rice using the instructions on page 89, and prepare the sushi rolls in the same way, without the strips of marinated tuna.

5 Place a mussel on each roll and spoon over some of the juices and shallots. Sprinkle with roasted sesame seeds and serve immediately with shoyu sauce and wasabi.

steven says

AT TIMES I FEEL LIKE PICASSO WITH FOOD; I spray or brush coloured oils over plates, or I create something unique. The trademark of a really talented cook is his or her creative flair. It is fun to play with food – try experimenting with your own tastes and garnishes for sushi, using seafood, smoked salmon and flavoursome mushrooms.

baked tamarillo with coconut and lemongrass ice

FOR THE COCONUT AND LEMONGRASS ICE

240 ml coconut milk

½ vanilla pod

1 stick of lemongrass, split in half
   lengthways

3 egg yolks

50 g caster sugar

6 tbsp desiccated coconut

FOR THE BAKED TAMARILLO

2 large tamarillo fruits

120 g brown raw cane sugar

50 ml sweet white wine

100 ml orange juice

icing sugar to serve (optional)

1 In a saucepan, bring the coconut milk, vanilla pod and lemongrass to the boil over high heat.

2 In a bowl, whisk the yolks and sugar until creamy. Stir in 3 tbsp of the coconut, and then pour in the boiling coconut milk. Remove the vanilla pod and lemongrass and keep to one side. Whisk the mixture continuously until light and frothy.

3 Rinse the saucepan and pour the mixture back into it. Simmer over a low heat, stirring continuously. When the mixture has thickened enough to coat a spoon – about 20 minutes – remove from the heat. Set aside and allow to cool, then sieve the mixture to remove any lumps.

4 If you have one, pour the mixture into an ice-cream maker. Otherwise, pour into a well-chilled glass bowl and freeze, taking the ice cream out of the freezer every 30–45 minutes for a thorough stir for the first 2–3 hours.

5 When the ice cream is sufficiently frozen, coat 4 shaped moulds with the remainder of the dessicated coconut and then press the ice cream into each mould. Return them to the freezer for 30 minutes, then remove from the moulds and roll the shapes in dessicated coconut. Return the coated shapes to the freezer to keep them chilled until ready to serve.

6 Preheat the oven to 170°C. Cut each tamarillo fruit in half, leaving the stalks intact, and place them, cut side uppermost, in a deep ovenproof dish. Sprinkle the fruit with the sugar, and cover with the wine and orange juice, making sure that each fruit has an even coating of both. Bake in the oven for 15–20 minutes, or until the fruit flesh is juicy and tender.

7 Transfer the cooked fruit to warmed serving plates and serve hot, dusted with a little icing sugar, if you are using it, and accompanied by a portion of the coconut and lemongrass ice cream.

unite the home with family harmony

The aim of cultivating family harmony is to find ways to enjoy and make the most of each other's company. Being able to have fun together and build up positive mutual experiences will make for happy memories and a stronger bond between close relatives.

Each member of the family will have unique needs and characters, so Feng Shui aims to create an environment and menu that suits everyone and each role in the greater unit.

MENU PLANNING

Meals should be served at regular times and in a place where everyone can sit around the table together to ensure regular contact between all the members of the family. Foods that encourage family harmony are wholesome dishes that can be eaten together. Steven's braised lemon cod is a good example. Try to use foods

SHARING A FAMILY MEAL PROVIDES A PERFECT OPPORTUNITY TO BRING A SPECIAL BOND TO YOUR FAMILY. ENSURE THAT THE ENERGY FLOWS POSITIVELY BY CONSIDERING THE NEEDS OF EACH FAMILY MEMBER AND ENCOURAGING THEM TO APPRECIATE THE SENSE OF FAMILY UNITY. A YIN ATMOSPHERE IS PREFERABLE, WITH REVITALISING TREE ENERGY AND COMFORTING SOIL ENERGY.

that will not be extreme in terms of yin and yang and that are not overly stimulating or spicy. Yin foods with a high sugar content disrupt blood sugar levels and can increase the risk of emotional upsets. Yang foods that are high in saturated fats can make people feel more irritable and hot tempered.

Baked foods have a relatively metal chi energy, which encourages chi energies to move together, helping to create a close family unit. The braised lemon cod is designed to be light, wholesome and low in fats. The barley is high in complex carbohydrates and provides a healthy dish that everyone can share.

The cherry pie with coconut pastry also helps to promote closeness. The ingredients and the process of baking give it a greater proportion of soil energy. To encourage even greater family harmony, avoid using icing sugar or caster sugar in the pastry.

Freshly brewed tea is ideal for family situations, providing warmth and comfort without being overly stimulating. Earl grey would be a good choice, although you should try camomile if you want a soothing alternative. Japanese bancha twig tea aids digestion and can help you relax. It is also suitable for children – mix it with organic apple juice for a refreshing drink.

YOUR SURROUNDINGS

Where you live and eat has a great impact on the way you get on as a family. Tensions, arguments and major upsets are more likely to occur if your environment is cluttered, overly colourful or has too many hard or shiny surfaces, such as mirrors. These produce a faster flow of chi energy and make it hard to relax. Wooden furniture and floors have plenty of wholesome and revitalising tree energy, excellent for family health and harmony.

The best colours for a calming chi energy are pale yellow, cream, pale green and pink. Yellow is a harmonious colour that is associated with homes, families and food. There are many shades of yellow, so choose pale yin shades to retain a relaxing atmosphere, or strong, bright yellows if you want a more energising yang ambience. Cream is a relaxing background colour and green can add a refreshing lift to a room, generally in a relaxing manner. Use light, pastel shades to create a peaceful yin effect. Pink is associated with pleasure, fun and feeling content. Use it in small quantities to enhance joy and happiness.

family menu

BRAISED LEMON
COD WITH WHOLE
BARLEY AND
VANILLA

CHERRY PIE WITH
COCONUT PASTRY

serves 4

THE SUN STREAMING IN THROUGH THE HOME IS ESSENTIAL TO A HEALTHY AND HAPPY FAMILY. IT REFRESHES THE CHI ENERGY, DISSIPATES DAMP OR STAGNATING CHI AND MAKES YOU FEEL ALIVE AND HAPPY. THE BEST SOURCES OF SUNLIGHT ARE FROM THE SOUTH-WEST, WEST OR NORTH-WEST, BRINGING THE SETTLED AND HARMONIOUS AFTERNOON AND EVENING LIGHT. ALTERNATIVELY, LIGHT FROM THE SUNRISE IN THE SOUTH-EAST PROVIDES ACTIVE CHI, ENCOURAGING YOU TO DO MORE TOGETHER.

Inspiring vitality and growth, plants can introduce a positive energy to family life. The best plants for creating a relaxing yin atmosphere are those with large, floppy or rounded leaves, such as rubber plants. Spiky leaves create a dynamic yang atmosphere and are better suited to large, open spaces.

SEATING PLAN

Someone facing south-west, the direction of the afternoon, will enjoy the chi energy associated with togetherness. West, the direction of the setting sun, is helpful for feeling content and enjoying the company of others. Facing north-west helps you to feel in control and better able to deal with conflicts. Alternatively, facing north aligns you with the chi energy associated with the night and winter, and is good for keeping calm and peaceful. If you are facing south-east, the chi energy associated with communication can help you to be active while maintaining harmony among the family members.

Choose the directions that are best for each family member. If one person tends to be confrontational the chi energy of the north is more calming. Conversely, an overly serious person may benefit from the more playful and relaxed west-facing position. Facing north-west is ideal for reasserting parental authority, while south-west is best if you feel you are drifting apart. South-east would be best if you are bored and lack stimulation.

PHOTOGRAPHS Family unity can be strengthened by decorating the room with harmonious or happy family photographs.

steven says

WHEN I ENTERTAIN THE FAMILY I choose dishes that are relatively easy to prepare and cook, and food that will fill the home with wonderful aromas. Baked dishes are ideal for sharing, and they have a warming and comforting feel. On this occasion, I chose white fish to suit a family luncheon with scented rice. Cook a whole fish if you want to bring the family really close – my salmon recipe on page 137 is wonderfully satisfying. The home-made cherry pie is a real treat, adding a lovely tart sweetness at the end. Both recipes are for four people, so multiply the ingredients if you have a large family. The results will be perfect for bringing the family together and stimulating a lovely warm atmosphere.

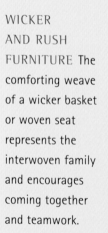

WICKER AND RUSH FURNITURE The comforting weave of a wicker basket or woven seat represents the interwoven family and encourages coming together and teamwork.

table setting

ALTHOUGH THE FAMILY EATING ROOM should be kept casual and relaxed, it is also essential that you set the table to encourage harmonious feelings. A round or oval table enables everyone to see each other and makes it easier to talk and discuss family issues. A wooden table or one covered with a pale linen tablecloth makes the atmosphere relatively yin. Avoid glass, metal or stone-topped tables as these create a yang energy that increases the risk of arguments.

Try not to crowd the table with too many items. Open spaces on the surfaces make it easier to eat together without feeling fractious and irritable. Wooden cutlery encourages chi energy to move slowly, creating a relaxing atmosphere and matt surfaces, such as a soft fabric tablecloth, notably linen, absorb chi energy, also slowing it and making the atmosphere less tense. Choose crockery and napkins in cream, pale yellow, pale blue, pale green or pink in order to increase yin chi energy. This will make it easier for you to enjoy each others' company without tension. Try wooden plates if you want something different in a more yin material.

Choose cheerful flowers, such as daisies, daffodils, dianthus and sunflowers. The best colours are creams, pale yellows or pinks.

HOME-MADE ITEMS Create a homely feeling by decorating the dining area with home-made items, such as curtains, soft furnishings and other decorative features in colours that enhance family harmony. If you have children, you may want to display some of their handiwork.

braised lemon cod with whole barley and vanilla

200 g whole barley

1 large carrot, peeled and shredded

1 large leek, shredded

1 small onion, peeled and shredded

4 cloves garlic, peeled and
    chopped

salt and freshly milled black pepper

800 g cod (or another white fish),
    skinned and boned and
    divided into 4 portions

2 unwaxed lemons, thinly sliced

1 sprig of thyme

1 bay leaf

2 pieces star anise

1 vanilla pod, sliced in half
    lengthways

1½ litres fish stock (see page 150)

100 ml white wine

juice of 1 lemon

200 ml crème fraîche (low fat)

2 tbsp chopped fresh chervil
    (or fennel herb)

1 Preheat the oven to 150°C. Blanch the barley in a pan of boiling water over a medium heat for 15 minutes, then remove, drain and immediately refresh in cold water. Drain again, pat dry and set aside.

2 Cover the bottom of a deep oven-proof baking dish with the shredded carrot, leek, onion and chopped garlic. Season well and then sprinkle with barley. Place the fish on top and season well. Cover the fish with the slices of lemon and add the thyme, bay leaf, star anise and vanilla. Cover with the warm fish stock and finally cover with aluminium foil, pierce it and bake in the oven until the fish is cooked, approximately 30–40 minutes. Test by easing the point of a sharp knife into the centre of a thick piece of fish; if it goes in easily, it is cooked.

3 Retaining the vegetables and barley with the fish, strain away the remaining juices with a ladle and pass the juice through a fine sieve into a clean saucepan. Place it over a high heat and stir in the white wine and lemon juice. Add the vanilla pod from the baking dish. Reduce for 5 minutes, then spoon in the crème fraîche. Continue to reduce for a further 5 minutes. Meanwhile, keep the fish warm by covering the dish with the foil.

4 Taste the sauce, season and add the chervil or fennel herb. Pour the sauce around the fish and barley in the baking dish. Remove the thyme, bay leaf, vanilla pod and star anise. Take the dish to the table and serve with mashed potatoes or spiced rice and some lightly cooked fresh green vegetables.

cherry pie with coconut pastry

FOR THE PASTRY

225 g plain flour

pinch of salt

150 g desiccated coconut

125 g unsalted butter, soft

1 egg, beaten

FOR THE FILLING

400 ml red wine

1 tsp ground cinnamon

400 g fresh cherries, stoned

1 heaped tbsp cornflour

juice of 1 lemon

100 g desiccated coconut

1 egg white, beaten for glaze

icing sugar to serve (optional)

1 To make the pastry, sift the flour and salt into a bowl. Add the coconut and butter and mix together with your fingers (or in a food mixer). Gradually add the egg and mix until the pastry is well-blended and firm enough to form a ball (if it is too dry to hold together, add a little cold water). Wrap in clingfilm and chill for 1 hour.

2 Preheat the oven to 220°C. Reserve a third of the pastry for the lid, and roll out the rest until it is thin enough to line a buttered and floured pie tin approximately 20.5 cm in diameter (preferably with a removable base). Prick the pastry with a fork and bake blind in the oven for approximately 10 minutes, then remove from the oven and set aside. Reduce the oven temperature to 190°C.

3 Meanwhile, prepare the filling. Heat the red wine in a saucepan over a low heat with the cinnamon and then add the cherries. Cook gently for about 20 minutes until the cherries are soft and tender. Mix the cornflour with a little water and pour into the hot cherries; stir well and remove from the heat. Add the lemon juice and cool.

4 Sprinkle the base of the cooked pastry with the desiccated coconut and pour the cooled filling into the pastry base. Roll out the lid and cover the pie, cutting the excess from around the edge and pressing the edges of the lid to the case to seal. Pierce the lid with a skewer. Brush with egg white. Bake in the oven for 30-40 minutes until the pastry is golden brown.

5 Gently turn the pie out of the tin and place it on a serving dish. Dust the top with icing sugar, if you are using it, and serve with warm custard (see page 152).

charge your evening with passion

AROUSE YOUR EMOTIONS AND THOSE OF YOUR DINNER GUEST WITH STRONG YANG CHI ENERGY, SPINNING QUICKLY TO GENERATE PASSION AND TO PROVIDE A SENSUAL MOOD FOR YOUR MEAL. USE THE ELEMENT OF FIRE TO BRING DEEPER EMOTIONS TO THE SURFACE AND TO ENCOURAGE SELF-EXPRESSION, INSPIRING AN ELEMENT OF SPONTANEITY.

Passion is often accompanied by a fiery, warm feeling deep inside; it is an emotion that can be long lasting, leading to a devotion to a lover, child or hobby.

Your menu and the atmosphere in which you eat can greatly increase your existing feelings of passion. This can be done by using fast-flowing yang energy, with plenty of light and reflective surfaces to enhance the feeling of light and movement. You cannot, however, generate feelings of passion from nowhere, and the element of fire can help this. Fire energy has the effect of moving chi energy from deep inside the body outward to the surface. It also is the element responsible for sensuality and strong feelings.

If you want to be passionate with someone, make sure that the feeling is reciprocal; your dinner guest may become bewildered, angry or upset if you misjudge the situation!

MENU PLANNING

Fire up your meals with spicy foods, fried foods and foods cooked on a high flame, helping you to feel and express your emotions. Steven has chosen two relatively light recipes – a main course and a dessert – to inflame your meal without leaving you too full for fun.

Instead of a starter, you can relax and warm your spirits for the evening with a cocktail. A red cocktail with strong, fruity flavours will provide a dramatic introduction to the evening. Tomato juice with vodka makes a tasty Bloody Mary; perfect for striking a passionate chord. Alternatively, mix red grapefruit juice, cranberry juice or blackcurrant with your favourite spirit, or make a concoction of your own. A sparkling drink sends an extra spin into the ambient chi energy, creating a mood for playfulness and frivolity. Champagne is also auspicious for the occasion.

Steven's menu starts with the sizzling marlin brochettes, with plenty of great pungent flavours. Garlic stimulates your senses; if eaten on a regular basis, garlic can help you to feel more emotional, although you should be careful not to eat too much garlic if you are prone to emotional upset. The chilli has a great fire energy, stirring up the chi energy deep inside your body and bringing it up to the surface. Cook this dish by stirring it quickly in the wok over a high flame to add more fire energy, and serve it straight away while still scorching hot.

Similarly, the crêpes suzettes with sambuca are prepared in a frying pan over a flame – a sizzling hot dish, especially if you set alight to it. The sambuca adds more fire chi energy.

Accompany your meal with some hot sake to help you feel warm inside while also increasing your emotional intensity. If you would prefer not to drink alcohol, try an iced fruit juice instead, with a splash of sparkling mineral water. Drinking liqueurs, such as cognac, at the end of your meal will fill you with an ardent glow.

THE SETTING

To generate greater passion, you must find ways to stir up the energy in your dining room, making the chi spin faster and with more feeling. Open fires, candles, moving mobiles or a small fountain all can add a quality of movement to the proceedings. Bright colours, especially bright purple and hot pink, add to the passionate atmosphere. Make sure that there is no stagnating chi in the room – in corners where there is no air movement – and if possible avoid eating in a basement or a room with little natural light.

A bright, fiery purple is the ideal colour for passion and purple napkins or flowers add vivacity to the atmosphere. Set the table with muted background colours – a pale green or cream –

NAKED FLAMES ARE CERTAIN TO BRING AN EXTRA BLAZE OF PASSION TO A MEAL. YOU CAN INCREASE THE FIRE ELEMENT AFTER THE MEAL BY SERVING FLAMING LIQUEURS, SUCH AS SAMBUCA, WITH COFFEE.

a passionate menu

SIZZLING MARLIN BROCHETTES WITH TEMPEH AND BEANS

CRÊPES SUZETTES WITH SAMBUCA

serves 2

in all the crockery and in the serving dishes so that the purple stands out. A real open fire adds strong and fierce fire chi to the room, putting you in the mood for sensuality. If you don't have a fire, introduce warm, fiery colours to the room, such as purple and red. Cooking the food at the table or serving a flambé dish adds fire, certain to encourage passion and strong feelings.

The flickering orange and yellow light of candles sends powerful emotional energy into the room. Choose purple and red colours and star-shaped holders to stimulate fire energy. Alternatively, use wooden holders as the tree energy will support the fire energy.

Mirrors help to spin chi energy around faster, but too many mirrors or too large a mirror can make the room feel overly stimulating.

Bright, indirect lighting adds vitality, but avoid the glare of light bulbs by directing them toward the corners of the room. Moving images projected onto a white wall add a feeling of emotional movement, especially if they are colourful and the subjects are sensual.

Bright purple, red or yellow flowers can add dynamic yang energy. Flowers that spread out or have a star shape, such as clematis, generate fire energy and can enhance desire. Similarly, plants that grow upwards, especially those with pointed leaves, such as a yucca, provide plenty of invigorating fire energy.

Silk is particularly voluptuous, especially if it is slightly shimmering. Bright purple is the ideal colour, although bright pink and cream also can set off the right ambience. Try draping silk over existing curtains or over the backs of your chairs.

SEATING PLAN

Expose yourself to more enticing chi energy by sitting facing south – the midday direction. This bright, radiant chi energy encourages passionate emotions. If your dining room layout doesn't allow this, face south-west for increased intimacy, west when you're seeking a playful, mutually pleasurable atmosphere, or south-east to encourage conversation. South-east would also be helpful if you are trying to muster greater confidence for a creative pursuit.

table setting

IDEALLY, USE A WOODEN TABLE with a polished surface to speed emotional energy around the room, although a metal or glass shiny surface will have a similar effect. If you don't have a shiny table, use a tablecloth in a solid, bright colour, such as purple or red, or in a crisp white. If your table has extensions, make it as large as possible, giving space for your chi energy fields to expand. A long, rectangular table, representing tree chi energy, will support the fiery chi energy of passion.

Low, comfortable, upholstered chairs are best suited for passionate dining; cushions scattered on the floor around a low table add an exotic air to the proceedings. However, the chi energy would move slowly around you and you would need to introduce plenty of bright colours to keep the overall atmosphere yang.

Dazzling cutlery in silver or steel will spin the chi faster and send sparkles around the room as you eat. Match it with other metal objects on the table, such as silver salt and pepper shakers and serving dishes.

SILK CUSHIONS

Keep the chi energy spinning fast by using soft furnishings with shiny surfaces. Cushions made from silk or satin, preferably in bright purples and pinks, can imbue the atmosphere with a voluptuous, ostentatious ambience.

BRASS FITTINGS Polished brass door handles and other room fixtures stimulate fast-moving chi energy, as well as being visually stimulating.

PICTURES of nudes or partially clothed figures can stimulate the senses. Strong oil paintings with plenty of movement, texture and colour are powerful and can evoke powerful feelings.

sizzling marlin brochettes with tempeh and french beans

FOR THE MARLIN BROCHETTES

350 g marlin steak (or tuna fish)

150 ml light olive oil

1 sprig rosemary

2 cloves garlic, peeled and crushed

4 sticks of lemongrass

4 bay leaves (optional)

FOR THE TEMPEH

400 g tempeh or tofu

1 red onion, finely chopped

1 red scotch bonnet or West Indian chilli, deseeded and finely chopped

200 g French beans

1 tsp tamarind syrup

1 tsp garam masala, freshly ground if possible (see page 149)

fresh coriander to garnish

1 Cut the marlin or tuna into 4 cm cubes and cover with the oil, rosemary and garlic. Season well with salt and freshly milled black pepper and leave in the refrigerator to chill for a minimum of 30 minutes, a maximum of 10 hours.

2 Remove the fish cubes, reserving the marinade, and skewer them onto the lemongrass sticks – about 3 cubes per portion. Skewer a bay leaf onto the end of each lemon grass stick if you like.

3 Cut the tempeh or tofu into 4 cm cubes. Heat 1 tbsp of the marinade in a wok over a high heat and fry the onion and the chilli for 5 minutes, until coloured but not brown. Add the tempeh and fry, keeping it moving, for a further 30 seconds until the outsides of the tempeh cubes are coloured. Remove the tempeh and reserve.

4 Prepare the beans by blanching them in salted boiling water for 2 minutes, refresh and drain. Place the beans, tamarind syrup and garam masala into the wok and cook for 3–4 minutes. If necessary, add more of the marinade oil to the wok to help soften the beans, but be careful not to colour them too much.

5 Put the tempeh back into the wok for a further 2 minutes. Taste and season. Remove from the heat, transfer to a serving dish and keep warm.

6 To cook the marlin, place the skewers on a chargrill, griddle or under a hot grill and cook for 30 seconds on each side, 2 minutes in total. Each cube should be pink in the centre. Remove, season and serve with the spiced tempeh and French beans with a coriander garnish.

crêpes suzettes with sambuca

FOR THE CRÊPES

2 eggs

250 ml milk

100 g plain flour, sifted

dash of olive oil

pinch of salt

vegetable oil for frying

FOR THE FLAMBÉ SAUCE

55 g unsalted butter

100 g maple syrup

juice and zest of 2 unwaxed oranges

50 ml sambuca or Pernod

1 Prepare the pancake batter in the usual way by whisking together the eggs, milk, flour, olive oil and salt. Pass the mixture through a sieve to extract any lumps.

2 Heat a crêpe pan or large frying pan over a medium heat, cover the base with a little vegetable oil and pour off any surplus. Ladle enough pancake batter into the pan to cover the base thinly. Cook for about a minute on each side, until brown. Fold into quarters in the frying pan, remove and set to one side. Make 2–3 pancakes per portion.

3 Next, you need to prepare the flambé sauce. In a separate pan, melt the butter over a medium heat and add the maple syrup, the orange juice and zest and stir well. Continue to cook for about 5 minutes until the sauce reduces and thickens.

4 Add the pancakes one by one into the sauce. Once they are all in the pan, pour in the sambuca, tipping the pan into the flame to ignite it (or heat a ladle and ignite the sambuca if you have no gas). Serve immediately with the sauce still flaming.

fun and healthy mealtimes for children

The best start you can give your children in life is to feed them natural, healthy, nutritious foods. If they develop a taste for vegetables, grains and fruit early on, it may make it easier for them to avoid junk food later. Part of the secret to achieving this is to find natural foods that you can prepare in a way that children will enjoy.

MENU PLANNING

Get your children used to having grains and vegetables with every meal. A well-balanced meal, including a soup, a main course and a healthy dessert, will make a good foundation for future years.

Steven's simple tomato soup is fresh and tasty. It is a yin dish, creating a calming and pacifying start to the meal. If your children don't like tomatoes, try other vegetables such as carrots, watercress or cauliflower.

MEALTIMES FOR CHILDREN SHOULD IDEALLY COMBINE FUN WITH A CERTAIN MEASURE OF FORMALITY AND CALM. YOU CAN SUIT YOUR CHILDREN'S INDIVIDUAL NEEDS BY ADJUSTING THE BALANCE OF YIN AND YANG AND THE FIVE ELEMENTS IN BOTH THE DINING AREA AND THE FOOD YOU SERVE, WHICH ENABLES YOU TO BRING OUT THE BEST IN YOUR CHILDREN.

The baked bean croquettes are always popular with my children and are good sources of protein. Beans contain a range of nutrients. To gain the maximum health benefit, choose organic, sugar-free baked beans. This dish will be relatively yang. If you wish to reduce the fat content, use tofu instead of cheese.

The baked bananas are a sweet and satisfying dish for children. The ingredients are primarily yin, although the baking process adds a yang energy, balancing the dish and making it more hearty.

Healthy drinks to accompany the meal include spring water or fresh, organic fruit juice, both of which provide a pure yin fluid refreshment. Too much water consumed throughout a meal can slow digestion because it dilutes the digestive enzymes in the stomach. Encourage children to drink more fluids at other times if you find they are thirsty during meals

Regular meals served at the same time each day will help your children to get used to a biological rhythm, making it easier for them to eat and digest well.

HEALTHY SNACKS FOR CHILDREN

Children need to eat more frequently than adults and a variety of healthy snacks are available to keep their energy levels up between meals. The main idea is to avoid giving them snacks that are high in salt, sugar, unnatural flavourings and saturated fats, all of which are unhealthy. You may need to allow your children's palate to change so they can enjoy the more simple tastes of natural foods; too many sugary or fried snacks can reduce children's ability to enjoy the taste of healthy foods.

If you want to retain their appetite for their meals, use foods that are healthy and satisfying in the short term. Light yin snacks include fresh fruit and raisins. Bananas are high in fruit sugars and can be useful when your children are hungry, although make sure there is plenty of time before the next meal. Dried fruits, such as raisins and dried apricots, are more yang than fresh fruit and make an ideal travel snack. High in nutrients and fibre, they also contain large amounts of natural sugar that can be helpful for a child with a sweet tooth.

Roasted nuts and seeds are more yang than fruits and have a higher proportion of protein, but they can make children thirsty, so keep a drink on hand.

Sugar-free jams are useful for spreading on rice cakes, wholemeal bread or crumpets. There is also a wide range of sugar-free biscuits, waffles and sweets that generally have more healthy ingredients, although in excess these will certainly spoil a child's appetite and ability to enjoy more simple tastes.

THE SURROUNDINGS

Bright colours and shiny surfaces can be overstimulating, so natural woods and cotton fabrics in more subtle shades are ideal. Pale blue, pale green, cream and mauve all create a calming influence for bibs, napkins and tablecloths. Steer clear of bright or bold patterns that may distract the children from eating.

Wood encourages a natural and balanced chi energy, softer than metal but harder than fabric. A hard, dark wood, such as mahogany, is more formal and yang, suiting easily distracted children. A light, soft wood, such as pine, or a wicker or woven seat base is more yin, creating a quieter, friendlier atmosphere.

Children often love candles at the dinner table and these will keep their attention on the meal. For more everyday occasions, an overhead light directed at the centre of the table will keep the focus on the table top.

children's menu

SIMPLE TOMATO SOUP

BAKED BEAN
CROQUETTES

BAKED BANANAS WITH
ORANGE AND MAPLE
SYRUP

serves 4

SUGAR-FREE JAMS ON WHOLEMEAL BREAD OR RICE CAKES MAKE GOOD YANG SNACKS TO KEEP CHILDREN SATISFIED BETWEEN MEALS. ALTERNATIVELY, A PORTION OF FRESH OR DRIED FRUIT, OR ROASTED SEEDS AND NUTS ALL PROVIDE EXTRA NUTRIENTS FROM NATURAL SOURCES.

Keep a variety of leafy plants in your dining area, but avoid more yang spiky plants as they can make children restless, fidgety and overactive.

It is reassuring for children to be able to see their toys and possessions in the home. Try to display their favourite toys on a shelf or put soft toys around the room. The gentle movement of a mobile can be relaxing or arousing for a child. A more yang metal mobile should be placed in the west of a room, and a yin wooden mobile would be better in the east. Bright colours may be too distracting, so choose mellow, subtle shades and avoid hanging the mobile directly over the children or the table.

SEATING PLAN

Every child is different, so you need to consider which of the eight directions would be most helpful for each. A child that is prone to tantrums, for example, might benefit from facing west or north – playful or quiet respectively. However, the child will not behave well facing north-east or south, which encourage more competitive or emotional responses respectively. See the information on page 67 for the characteristics of each of the eight directions.

Ideally, parents should sit facing north-west and south-west, which are associated with the father and mother respectively. If this is not possible, a parent should sit facing south-east.

Avoid seating children with their backs to a door or other distractions – this tends to make them feel restless and less likely to settle down.

table setting

SOME CHILDREN RESPOND POSITIVELY to a formal table setting and find it easier to behave well. You may find your child develops a respect for the occasion of formal mealtimes, and enjoys the sense of ritual and routine. A very casual yin setting increases the risk of children taking the meal less seriously and messing around.

Ideally, the chairs should be high and upright to reduce the temptation for children to get off their chairs and run around during the meal. A highchair for younger children helps them to get into the habit of staying in one place for the duration of the meal and focuses their attention on eating.

Try to avoid plastic plates or cups as they do not encourage a natural flow of chi energy; china, glass or enamel offer better chi energy for small children. In my opinion, children should be trusted with breakable china plates as early as possible to provide a sense of responsibility. This will also encourage them to take mealtimes more seriously. Children can use small metal or wooden knives, forks and spoons, although you must make sure these are not sharp. Avoid plastic cutlery.

ART If your children enjoy creating works of art, hang the pictures in your home to reinforce a sense of achievement. Ideally, any paintings you particularly like should be framed and displayed.

WOOD Natural wood furniture and decorations promote growth, vitality without overstimulating the environment. Use wooden ornaments and objects to add a calming yin energy to the meal.

WINDCHIMES The sporadic sound created by a windchime adds an enchantment to the atmosphere, especially if it is a high-pitched, metallic ring with several different notes. Windchimes purify chi energy and bring fresh, vital chi to a room.

TOYS If you can keep toys tidy and orderly, it will help your children respect them and their own space in the home, and encourage a calm orderliness to family gatherings, such as meal times.

simple tomato soup

1 tbsp grape seed oil
1 clove garlic, peeled and crushed
1 medium onion, sliced thinly
675 g vine tomatoes, cut into quarters
150 ml clear vegetable stock (see
    page 150) or boiling water
salt and freshly milled black pepper
1 tbsp chopped fresh basil (optional)

1 Heat the oil in a pan over a medium
heat, and gently fry the garlic and
onions for 5 minutes, until the onions
are transparent but not brown. Add the
tomatoes with their skins and seeds,
and toss them with the fried onions.

2 Add the stock or water and stir
well. Put the lid on the saucepan
and simmer for 20 minutes.

3 Pour the tomato mixture into a
food processor and blend to a
purée. Pour the purée through a fine
sieve to extract the skins and seeds,
pressing with the back of a spoon.

4 Season to taste. If the tomatoes are
not very ripe, add the juice of an
orange or a tablespoon of honey to help
sweeten the flavours. Finish with
chopped fresh basil (optional).

baked bean croquettes

4 heaped tbsp sugar-free baked beans,
    drained
2 tbsp tofu or grated mild cheddar
    cheese
2 potatoes, peeled, boiled and mashed
1 egg yolk
1 tbsp chopped fresh parsley
salt and freshly milled black pepper
6–8 tbsp soft white breadcrumbs
50 g plain flour
1 egg, whisked for egg wash
2–3 tbsp grape seed oil for frying

1 Mix together the beans, tofu or
cheese, mashed potato and egg
yolk. Add the parsley and seasoning.

2 Mould into 8 croquette shapes. If
the mixture is a little wet, mix in a
tablespoon of breadcrumbs.

3 Dip each croquette first into the
flour, then the egg wash and finally
coat with the breadcrumbs.

4 Heat the oil in a frying pan over
a high heat and fry the croquettes
until golden brown on both sides.

5 If, like my kids, your children love
cheese, melt a little over the top of
each croquette. Or you can add a
helping of voodoo salsa or orange and
tomato coulis (both recipes can be
found on page 151). Serve with green
vegetables, such as broccoli or cabbage,
and a wholemeal roll.

baked bananas
with orange and maple syrup

4 ripe bananas
60 g unsalted butter
juice of 1 large orange
50 ml maple syrup
natural yoghurt, to serve on side
    (optional)

1 Preheat the oven to 200°C. Peel the bananas and cut the flesh in half, lengthways. Place, cut side up, in a baking dish.

2 Melt the butter in a saucepan over low heat and add the orange juice and maple syrup. Mix in well until smooth. Taste and adjust the sweetness if necessary by adding more maple syrup or more orange juice.

3 Pour the orange and maple syrup mixture over the bananas and bake in the oven for 7–10 minutes. Allow the bananas to cool a little in the baking dish, then place 2 halves of banana into each bowl and spoon over some of the orange and maple syrup mixture. You can serve baked bananas on their own or with a teaspoonful of natural organic yoghurt.

steven says

I HAVE ALWAYS FED MY TWO GIRLS, SERENA 10 AND STEFANIE 7, the best and freshest of foods – and it shows in their health and vitality. It is amazing what you can do quickly and easily with fresh ingredients – busy mums and dads really don't have to rely on pre-prepared or convenience products if they know a couple of quick recipes. My simple tomato soup is a very popular recipe with both the kids and the parents. Taking responsibility, and caring, for your child's health includes knowing exactly what you are giving them to eat and drink, even if cooking for health sometimes means careful shopping, spending a little more money on organic foods, or even growing your own for extra freshness.

create a surge of excitement

A MEAL FOR EXCITEMENT COULD BE USED TO PROVOKE ADVENTURE OR PROVIDE MOTIVATION FOR A JOB OR TASK. YOU MAY BE CELEBRATING AN ACHIEVEMENT OR SUCCESS, OR SIMPLY FEEL A JOIE DE VIVRE THAT YOU WANT TO SHARE WITH YOUR FRIENDS. FAST YANG ENERGY HELPS TO CREATE THE SCENE, WITH PLENTY OF VITAL TREE ENERGY AND THE WARMTH OF FIRE.

Feelings of excitement about somebody or something are often accompanied by increased energy levels, possibly a tingling sensation and a surge of enthusiasm. Each person will have specific things that bring feelings of excitement, whether it's sports, activities, friends, decorating your home, the opportunity to make money or buying new clothes.

MENU PLANNING

Choose yang foods to speed up the movement of chi energy around your body. Strong flavours and hot foods create the perfect cocktail for frivolity, especially if you fry foods – the best cooking method for stimulating fire energy. You can also build up invigorating tree energy by including plenty of fresh vegetables, raw, steamed or blanched. To feel excited, the foods need to be light – heavy foods can draw chi energy into your abdomen. Combine Steven's recipes with other light foods, such as broccoli, cauliflower, spring onions, leeks, chinese leaves and parsley. Natural sauerkraut will help to make the fried foods more digestible.

The fried lentil cakes with cumin combine the stimulating properties of chillies and cumin with the more stable chi energy of the lentils. Like the onion bhaji, the frying process adds more of that essential fire energy.

The stir-fry combines the crisp yin vegetables with the fire energy in the frying process, putting you in an aroused state of mind. This dish is light way to satisfy your tastebuds without feeling too full. This is complemented by the wild mushrooms in giant pasta shells with the delicious red onion marmalade providing a satisfying, flavoursome yang dish.

The green chilli sauce for the vermicelli fried king prawns has a great burst of flavours for sparking excitement. The peppers, garlic and coriander will all stimulate your chi energy, making it easier to feel a rush of energy. Deep-frying the prawn mixture adds more fire energy to the food.

Any stimulating drink, such as coffee, peppermint tea or lemon and ginger tea, will give you more get up and go. Sake, whiskey or brandy are also good fiery drinks, although beer will help to balance the meal.

YOUR SURROUNDINGS

Your aim is to help chi energy move around your environment with more vigour and with stronger ebbs and flows. This is helped with bright colours, intense lighting, pointed shapes and hard, shiny, flat surfaces. Try to avoid clutter – over-furnished rooms or too many fabric surfaces slow the flow of chi energy and make the space feel too cosy for excitement.

Helpful, bright colours include purple, yellow and red, while vivid greens and blues can also be exciting. Intense halogen lighting speeds up the flow of chi energy. Generally, shiny marble, stone or wooden floors allow a smoother, faster passage of chi energy. Use blinds instead of curtains to help the chi energy flow easily. The blinds could be made of wood or metal, the latter providing a more yang energy.

Crystals reflect chi energy in all directions and in all the colours of the rainbow, boosting the excitement of the room and clearing stagnant chi. A crystal chandelier would be perfect, or if you don't have one as a main light, there are crystal decorated lampshades available for table or wall lamps.

Add more exciting fire chi energy with candles, using pointed or triangular shapes and the colour purple. If you are not using electric light, make sure that you have enough candles to make the room feel bright. Fire and water are opposites in Feng Shui and by putting them together – with floating candles in a bowl of water, for example – you can create a highly stimulating environment.

A variety of brightly coloured flowers can be visually stimulating, particularly if they are spiky. Purple thistles are excellent, as well as clematis and, to a lesser degree, tiger lilies. Place the flowers in a colourful container with a pointed shape, for example, a triangular, pyramid- or star-shaped vase.

Plants with pointed leaves generate fiery yang energy, with the result that the room feels more exciting. A yucca would be the ideal example. This could be made more effective with a spot light pointing up through its leaves and a mirror behind the plant to increase the flow of chi energy. Other examples of suitable plants would be palms or large ferns.

Choose paintings and ornaments, prints or posters that have bright colours and imagery inspiring thought – non-figurative or abstract, for example – that is not immediately obvious. Patterns and bold decorative designs also help to achieve this. You also could use images of something you find exciting, such as a sport, activity or event. Use fire chi energy shapes for sculptures or decorative objects – pyramids, star-shapes and triangles – to boost excitement.

SEATING PLAN

To expose yourself to exciting chi energy, sit so that you face one of the directions that relate to the rising sun – east, south-east or south. This bright, active chi energy will help to stimulate and uplift you. Of these, the south provides the strongest chi energy for excitement. Alternatively, north-east is good for greater motivation, or west for feeling more playful.

an exciting
menu

SPICY ONION BHAJI

WILD MUSHROOMS IN GIANT
PASTA SHELLS WITH RED ONION
MARMALADE

VERMICELLI FRIED KING PRAWNS
WITH GREEN CHILLI SAUCE

FRIED LENTIL CAKES
WITH CUMIN

HOT, STIR-FRIED
VEGETABLES

serves 4

table setting

THE MORE UNUSUAL THE
FURNITURE, the more interesting and
exciting it becomes. The table could be
unusually shaped, such as triangular,
which is associated with fire chi energy.
A square would be the next best choice.
A hard, shiny surface is also helpful,
particularly polished wood, glass,
marble or metal.

Ideally the chairs would be tall –
possibly even high stools – to inspire
vital tree energy. Tall chairs also lift
your head above the other furniture,
giving you access to the fast-moving
energy higher in the room. Wooden or
metal chairs encourage chi energy to
move more quickly and make it easier to
feel stimulated. If your chairs are
upholstered, try to choose a bright
colour or lay brightly coloured cloths or
napkins over paler shades.

For mats, crockery, glasses, napkins
and cutlery, bright colours and unusual
shapes increase the feeling of excitement. Leave a few open spaces on the
table top to allow chi
energy to move freely.
Any shiny surfaces
help the chi along, so
polish your cutlery,
plates, napkin holders
and glasses. Patterned
fabrics create a more
vital image, so choose
napkins, and table-
cloths with zig-zag or
triangular designs.

FIRE A roaring open fire generates energetic fire chi energy. Place a mirror over the fireplace to reflect more of the chi energy into the room. Keep the room well aerated and cool.

BRIGHT LIGHTING The most effective lighting for creating excitement would be bright and directional. Use the lighting to pick out some of the more interesting features in the room.

spicy onion bhaji

50 g chickpea flour and 65 g rice flour
    or 115 g plain or durum flour
¼ tsp bicarbonate of soda
½ tsp red chilli powder (cayenne)
½ tsp salt
250 ml milk
2 medium onions, peeled and thinly
    sliced
vegetable oil for deep-frying
pinch of curry powder

1 Mix together the flours, bicarbonate of soda, chilli powder and salt. Add the milk and whisk to a thick batter.

2 Add the onion and mould into balls, adding milk or flour as needed.

3 Preheat the oil to 170°C and deep-fry until golden brown. Season with a pinch of curry powder and serve.

wild mushrooms in giant pasta shells with red onion marmalade

FOR THE RED ONION MARMALADE
150 ml red wine
50 ml red wine vinegar
100 g brown unrefined sugar
2 medium red onions, sliced
salt and freshly milled
    black pepper

FOR THE WILD MUSHROOMS AND PASTA
½ tbsp light olive oil for frying
200 g wild mushrooms (or assorted),
    sliced
1 tbsp chopped fresh tarragon
salt and freshly milled black pepper
8 giant pasta shells, approximately
    10 cm in length

1 Prepare the red onion marmalade. Boil the red wine, vinegar and sugar. Reduce to simmering and add the onions. Cover and cook until the onions are translucent and the liquid absorbed, 20-30 minutes. Season and set aside.

2 Preheat the oven to 200°C. In a frying pan, heat the oil and add the mushrooms. Fry until tender, add the tarragon and remove from the heat.

3 Cook the giant pasta shells as instructed on the label. Drain and separate the shells and place them face up on a lightly oiled baking sheet.

4 Fill the pasta shells with the mushrooms, top with the onions and cover with baking foil to keep the pasta moist. Place in the oven for 5 minutes, and serve.

vermicelli fried king prawns with green chilli sauce

FOR THE GREEN CHILLI SAUCE

2 green peppers, deseeded and
    roughly chopped
1 shallot, peeled and chopped
1 clove garlic, peeled and chopped
2 green chillies, deseeded and
    chopped
2 tbsp chopped fresh coriander
150 ml coconut milk or clear vegetable
    stock (see page 150)
1 tbsp honey
salt and freshly milled black pepper
fresh lime juice to taste

FOR THE FRIED KING PRAWNS

8 large uncooked king prawns with
    shells
4 tbsp soft breadcrumbs

approximately 150 g of uncooked dried
    pasta linguine (as many colours
    and flavours as possible),
    shredded in a food processor
2 tbsp plain flour, seasoned
1 egg, beaten
vegetable oil for frying

1 Combine all the ingredients for the
green chilli sauce, without the lime
juice, in a saucepan over a gentle heat.
Simmer for 15–20 minutes, pour into a
liquidizer and blend until smooth. Pass
through a fine sieve, season and add
lime juice to taste. Set aside to cool.

2 Prepare the prawns by carefully
peeling off their shells, leaving the
tails intact. Slice the prawns in half
lengthways, but do not cut through the
tails, and open the body of the prawns
out flat for a butterfly effect. Remove
the membrane from the back.

3 Mix the breadcrumbs and the
uncooked pasta together. Toss the
prawns first in the flour, then in the
beaten egg and finally in the
breadcrumb and pasta mixture.

4 Preheat a pan of oil to 170°C
and deep-fry the coated prawns for
2–3 minutes, until golden brown.
Alternatively, shallow-fry them in a hot
wok for 2–3 minutes. Serve immediately
with the green chilli sauce.

fried lentil cakes with cumin

225 g dried lentils, any variety
850 ml clear vegetable stock (see
    page 150) or water
salt and freshly milled black pepper
2 green chillies, deseeded and sliced
1 medium onion, finely chopped
pinch of asafoetida
1 tbsp chopped fresh parsley
2 tsp cumin powder
½ tsp chilli powder
½ tsp salt
1 egg, beaten
2 tbsp fresh breadcrumbs
vegetable oil for frying

1 Bring the lentils to a boil in the vegetable stock and season. Reduce the heat, cover and simmer for 1 hour (or as instructed on label). Remove from the heat and blend in a food processor until relatively smooth.

2 Add the chillies, onion, asafoetida, parsley, cumin and chilli powder to the mixture and blend again.

3 Take 2 tablespoons of the mixture and mould into flat rissole shapes. Dip in beaten egg and then breadcrumbs and pan-fry in a little vegetable oil over a high heat for 3 minutes until crisp and golden.

hot, stir-fried vegetables

1 red pepper, deseeded and sliced
1 yellow pepper, deseeded
 and sliced
1 orange pepper, deseeded
 and sliced
200 g mangetout, sliced
100 g beansprouts
4 spring onions, cut in half
2 red chillies, deseeded and sliced
1 tbsp extra virgin olive oil
1 tbsp sesame oil
1 tbsp shoyu sauce
1 tbsp Thai fish sauce
1 tbsp toasted sesame seeds

1 Slice all the vegetables into batons, approximately 8 x 1 cm. Heat the olive oil and sesame oil in a wok over a high heat. Toss the vegetables and finely sliced chillies in the hot oil, then cook for 4 minutes, keeping the vegetables moving all the time to avoid burning.

2 Lower the heat and add the shoyu sauce and the Thai fish sauce. Mix well and turn onto the serving dish. Scatter the top with roasted sesame seeds.

restore the peace with reconciliation

MOST RELATIONSHIPS — WHETHER THEY ARE FAMILY, FRIENDS OR PARTNERS — FACE DIFFICULT PERIODS. RECOGNISING THE NEED FOR RECONCILIATION AND CREATING A SYMPATHETIC ATMOSPHERE FOR A MEAL CAN PROVIDE THE PERFECT WAY TO MAKE UP. USE CALMING YIN ENERGY AND THE ELEMENTS OF SOIL FOR SECURITY AND METAL FOR FEELING COMFORTABLE AND CONTENT.

Human relationships can so easily become beset with misunderstandings caused by harsh words said in the heat of the moment or petty arguments born out of personal frustration. At times these can lead to long-term resentments, seemingly irrevocable separations and utter breakdowns in communication. Conversely, some relationships simply fall apart due to a lack of attention and effort, with the result that people feel hurt, ignored and resentful. In certain situations, you may want to resolve differences from the past, enabling you to let go of any negative memories and the emotions that go with them.

MENU PLANNING

Foods that are soothing and calming are most likely to help you reconcile your differences, whereas sugary foods, strong spices or fried foods with a greater amount of fire energy, will increase the risk of a sudden flare up, heightening strong emotions and upsets. Bread and other baked foods can be helpful for bringing people closer together as the metal chi energy draws chi energy inward; try Steven's bread recipes on pages 154–5.

Steven's reconciliation recipes include spreads and accompaniments to eat with bread. The act of sharing bowls and serving dishes, rather than eating from individual plates, and mixing dishes with a variety of flavours compels you to feel closer and more sympathetic.

The felafel are a rich, tasty vegetarian dish that will help you to feel energetic while remaining relaxed and open. If you are particularly concerned with being calm and in control of your emotions, reduce the quantities of cumin seed and chilli powder so that the felafels are less spicy.

The chargrilled sardines add a strong yang element, especially with the high salt content and the process of chargrilling. Reduce the number you prepare – or miss them out completely – if someone present has a hot temper.

Hummus is a soothing, creamy spread that is ideal for re-settling situations, whereas the tapenade will be more yang with a salty taste that will help you to feel more in control and focused on self-disciplined.

The Lebanese-style tabbouleh salad is based on couscous or bulgar wheat, both high in complex carbohydrates, and therefore helpful for moderating your moods. The baked aubergine and garlic dip is rich and satisfying, making it easy to feel contented. The bruschetta will add a light and satisfying touch to the meal, however, if the garlic is too strong or applied too generously, this part of the meal will become more emotionally stimulating.

All of these dishes can be served with raw or blanched vegetables, such as carrots, cucumber, blanched watercress, mooli or radishes. You may want to finish with fresh fruits – soft, sweet fruits, such as melon, pears or apricots, would be ideal.

Hot apple juice, camomile tea, Japanese bancha twig tea, natural beers or still spring water are good, relaxing beverages.

YOUR SURROUNDINGS

To make it easier to restore peace with someone who feels angry or slighted you need to be calm and more receptive to their feelings and the spirit of reconciliation that you are trying to achieve. Show that you are prepared to listen and accept what has happened in the past. The energy that supports healing is yin and the elements soil, metal and water, so the room needs to feel soft, comfortable and relaxing.

It would be ideal to use colours associated with soil energy – yellow, beige and brown. In addition, incorporate plenty of soft fabrics, also associated with soil energy, to create a cosier and less confrontational atmosphere. Subtle patterns create a more peaceful image – use a checked pattern to increase soil energy, or wicker to imply a weaving together of spirits. Heavy, full-length curtains, wool carpets, wool rugs, tablecloths and soft chairs will all help. Use gentle, soft shapes – floor pillows, for example – and solid furniture to encourage chi energy to flow in a way that will promote closeness and forgiveness.

Low, indirect lighting would be most effective for creating an environment in which it is easier to come together. Bright or glaring lights can make you feel more on edge and stressed, risking confrontation. Use table lights set onto low tables to achieve a more cosy atmosphere. Either use cloth shades or a light that is reflected onto the wall. Incandescent lights have a slightly orange-coloured light which is calming. Mirrors make the room feel more yang, so take them down if you can, or drape a cloth over the top.

A fig tree can be grown so the stems are intertwined, symbolising coming together again. Alternatively, plant more than one plant in the same container to create an intertwining effect. Plants with rounded leaves will generate softer yin chi, making the room more peaceful.

It may also be beneficial to display photographs of times when you were happy together as a positive reminder of how much you can enjoy each other's company. The same idea would apply to mementos of things you achieved together, such as winning a competition, decorating a home or helping each other in your careers.

reconciliation menu

TABBOULEH SALAD

FELAFEL

CHARGRILLED SARDINES WITH GREEK SALAD

AUBERGINE AND GARLIC DIP

HUMMUS

BRUSCHETTA

TAPENADE

serves 4

table setting

IDEALLY THE CHAIRS SHOULD BE LOW AND COMFORTABLE. Upholstered chairs will encourage chi energy to slow down, making it easier to feel relaxed; choose paler soil colours, such as pale yellow. Ideally the table would be round, oval or at least have rounded corners to reduce the risk of directing fast-flowing chi energy through the room. A soft fabric tablecloth would help slow the flow of chi energy and offset the sharp corners. Again, choose calmer yin colours that are more relaxing.

Objects made from clay will add soil energy, subtly helping you overcome past difficulties. China spoons, napkin holders and china candlesticks can help to achieve this. Calming colours and curved shapes help to produce a more relaxing atmosphere. This would apply to mats, crockery, glasses, napkins and cutlery.

YELLOW FLOWERS Stimulate soil energy with a variety of yellow flowers, such as daffodils, chrysanthemums and sunflowers. Place these in the south-west of the room to improve harmony.

WOVEN MATS The soft, highly-textured weave in mats, wicker furniture and baskets gives them an energy that reinforces togetherness, teamwork and the ability to get along.

THICK RUGS Cover shiny floor surfaces with thick rugs to slow the flow of chi energy, encouraging mutual understanding.

tabbouleh salad

250 g bulgar wheat or couscous

3 shallots, finely chopped

3 spring onions, chopped

200 ml clear vegetable (or miso) stock (see page 150)

4 tbsp olive oil

4 tbsp lemon juice

1 tbsp chopped black olives

salt and freshly milled black pepper

4 tbsp chopped fresh parsley

1 tbsp chopped fresh mint

2 tbsp chopped fresh coriander

1 cos (or Webb's Wonder) lettuce

1 In a bowl, mix the bulgar wheat or couscous with the shallots and spring onions. Pour over the hot stock and soak until tender: 20 minutes for bulgar wheat, 5 minutes for couscous.

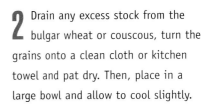

2 Drain any excess stock from the bulgar wheat or couscous, turn the grains onto a clean cloth or kitchen towel and pat dry. Then, place in a large bowl and allow to cool slightly.

3 Mix the oil and lemon juice together in a small dish with a fork, and pour into the bowl with the bulgar wheat or couscous. Stir in well.

4 Add the olives to the mixture and mix well – you can use vine tomatoes and cucumber for variety. Season to taste.

5 Mix the herbs into the mixture. Spread the lettuce leaves around the base and sides of the serving dish. Spoon the tabbouleh into the centre and serve.

steven says

THERE IS NOTHING QUITE AS COMFORTING AND WARMING AS THE aroma of freshly baked bread, and you can discover this wonderful art by turning to pages 154–5 for a variety of bread recipes that are simple and easy to prepare. Serve with dips, spreads, seafood and fresh fruit for a fantastic display of food – here are some of my favourite nibble-style meze dishes, inspired by the textures and flavours of the southern Mediterranean and Middle East.

felafel

125 g dried chickpeas or
    250 g canned chickpeas
1 medium onion, peeled and chopped
1 clove garlic, peeled
1 tsp chopped fresh parsley
½ tsp cumin seed
½ tsp coriander seed
1 tsp chopped fresh coriander
¼ tsp chilli powder
¼ tsp salt
¼ tsp freshly milled black pepper
¼ tsp baking powder
vegetable oil for frying

1 If you are using dried chickpeas, cover them with water and soak them for at least 8 hours. Then place them into a saucepan of water and simmer for a further 2 hours. Drain and leave to cool.

2 Blend the chickpeas in a food processor with the onion, garlic and the parsley until reasonably smooth. Add the spices, seasonings and the baking powder and blend well. Chill the mixture for 1–2 hours.

3 When chilled, take golf-ball-sized balls of the mixture, and then flatten them slightly into discs.

4 Heat the vegetable oil in a frying pan over a high heat and shallow fry the felafel on both sides until crisp, usually 1–2 minutes. Serve warm or chill for 1–2 hours and serve cold.

chargrilled sardines with greek salad

FOR THE GREEK SALAD
1 cos or romaine lettuce, chopped
1 tbsp mixed olives, stoned
2 tbsp chopped vine tomatoes
2 tbsp Feta cheese, in 1½ cm cubes
2 tbsp lemon juice
2 tbsp Greek olive oil
2 tbsp chopped fresh coriander
salt and freshly milled black pepper
FOR THE SARDINES
24 sardines, weighing about 30 g each
2 tbsp olive oil
coarse unrefined sea salt to cover
juice of 4 limes
2 limes for garnish

1 To prepare the Greek salad, mix all the ingredients and season to taste.

2 Heat your griddle pan or barbecue. Place the sardines on a baking tray or large plate and cover with the olive oil. Sprinkle sea salt over one side of the sardines, then flip over and repeat to coat the other side. Season with black pepper.

3 Grill the fish directly on the griddle or barbecue for approximately 2 minutes on each side. While they are cooking, squeeze on the lime juice.

4 Divide the Greek salad into equal portions and serve the sardines hot off the grill on top of the salad. Garnish each plate with half a lime and sprinkle liberally with chopped coriander.

aubergine and garlic dip

2 large aubergines, peeled
4 cloves garlic, peeled
salt and freshly milled black pepper
200–225 ml double cream
2 tbsp grated Parmesan cheese
squeeze of lemon juice

1 Preheat the oven to 200°C. Dice the aubergine flesh and slice the garlic. Place them in an oven-proof dish and season with a little salt and pepper. Pour over the cream, cover with foil and pierce a small hole in the foil.

2 Bake in the oven for 30 minutes, until the aubergine is soft and tender. Remove from the heat and blend in the food processor until smooth. Taste and season. If the mixture is too thin, add grated Parmesan cheese, then add the lemon juice and serve.

hummus

125 g chickpeas, dried
juice of 2 lemons
2 cloves garlic, peeled
2 tbsp olive oil
100 g tahini paste
salt and freshly milled black pepper

1 Cover the chickpeas with water and let them soak for at least 8 hours. Then simmer in a saucepan of water for a further 2 hours. Drain and cool.

2 Blend the chickpeas in a food processor with the lemon juice and garlic. Add the olive oil little by little, and then add the tahini in the same way. You should end up with a thick, creamy purée. If the mixture is too thick, add more olive oil. Season to taste and serve in a shallow dish.

bruschetta

6 plum tomatoes, skinned
1 bunch of fresh basil
1 ciabatta loaf
2 cloves garlic, peeled and halved
lots of extra virgin Italian
    olive oil
sea salt

1 Chop and mix the tomatoes and basil in a bowl and chill until the bread is hot and ready to serve.

2 Heat a griddle or grill. Cut the loaf into thick slices. Cook each slice until it is marked and criss-crossed on each side, or browned under the grill.

3 Remove the bread from the heat and rub the garlic onto the toasted bread. Drizzle with lots of olive oil, sprinkle with sea salt and serve topped with the tomato salad.

tapenade

4 whole anchovies, pickled in brine
1 tbsp black olives, stoned and
    roughly chopped
1 tbsp green olives, stoned and
    roughly chopped
1 tbsp chopped capers
2 tbsp chopped fresh parsley
juice of 1 lime
1 clove garlic, peeled and crushed
1 tbsp extra virgin olive oil
salt and freshly milled black pepper

1 If your anchovies are boned, cut them into halves lengthways and carefully remove and discard the bones. Break the remaining fish flesh into pieces with a fork.

2 Place the olives, capers and parsley in a large bowl and stir in the lime juice and garlic. Fold in the olive oil and the anchovies. Season to taste and serve.

special 4 occasions

When catering for a particular event, you will want to serve food that not only generates the perfect atmosphere for the occasion, but also complements the character of your guests and suits the external chi energy of the surroundings. This chapter provides tips on creating the best food and atmosphere for 8 different types of meal, ranging from a fun and hassle-free children's party to an important, once-in-a-lifetime event, such as a wedding.

ring the changes at a children's party

SIMON SAYS... Every child has unique needs and tastes, so the key to planning a children's party is to organise two different types of area that will between them satisfy the needs of everyone – a noisy, boisterous yang space, and a quiet, relaxing yin room.

The yang area is for fun and games. It is the ideal place to start the party, stimulating the children to interact and participate. Ensure it has as much empty space as possible for the children to play. An outdoor space in a garden or park would be ideal, although a large room can be made equally as stimulating. If the yang area is indoors, use bright colours and lighting to boost the yang energy, particularly with direct spotlights and coloured bulbs. Remove any unnecessary furniture, rugs or soft upholstery. Colourful balloons, soft sponge balls, mirrors and stimulating music all encourage children to be more physically active.

Ideally the children should eat in a quiet, yin space, returning to the yang atmosphere after a rest. The eating area should contain soft materials, indirect lighting and pastel shades. Large cushions on the floor, thick rugs and low, soft chairs create a secure atmosphere. Story telling, relaxing music and soft toys all help children to calm down.

THE SUCCESS OF THIS TYPE OF PARTY DEPENDS ON CREATING A SUFFICIENTLY YANG ATMOSPHERE TO ENCOURAGE THE YOUNG GUESTS TO TALK AND PLAY GAMES. HOWEVER, YOU NEED TO PREVENT IT FROM BECOMING TOO YANG, WHICH COULD LEAD TO OVER-EXCITEMENT AND, EVENTUALLY, TANTRUMS.

STEVEN SAYS... A birthday party is so important to a child, making him or her feel special for the day. But many parties are crammed with junk food, causing hyperactivity and temper tantrums – that familiar route to party hell! Choose the food for the party carefully; too many sugary items carry the risk of children becoming hyperactive as their blood-sugar levels increase rapidly. Try sugar-free jams, fruit juices and cordials, and provide plenty of complex carbohydrates, such as bread, pasta and vegetables, for slow-burning energy that prevents highs and lows.

The best approach is to sit down and make a list of a few simple but fresh and healthy ideas. You probably know the kinds of things your kids would enjoy. Make it a good mix of sweet and savoury, tasty nibbles and treats – it's pointless packing the table with healthy vegetables when we know that no one's interested.

Put some thought into the way that the food is presented; there's nothing that excites kids more than tantalising designs and brilliant colours. Hire or buy a few small cutters in animal shapes. Long cocktail sticks are marvellous for all sorts of cubes and small bites of things. Try a combination of apple, cherry tomatoes, melon balls, strawberries, cheddar cheese, cocktail pickled onions and chunks of banana. If you want to make a real spectacle, add a small chunk of chocolate in the middle.

SIMPLE SUGARLESS CAKE This is a quick-to-make cake for all occasions and it really doesn't contain any sugar! It is so easy that my youngest daughter has already mastered it, although she needs a little help with separating the eggs.

Preheat the oven to 200ºC. Separate 8 eggs and whisk the egg whites until they are stiff enough to form peaks. In a large bowl, whisk the yolks until they are creamy. Sift 200 g of self-raising flour into the yolks and stir well, then fold in the whites and stir well. Pour the mixture into a greased and floured cake tin, approximately 18 cm in diameter and 4 cm deep. Bake for 20–30 minutes until light brown.

Decorate however you want. Fresh fruit, sugar-free jam and whipped cream is my daughter's favourite, but for special occasions we cover the whole thing with a rich chocolate frosting made from 50 g of melted chocolate and 250 ml of whipped double cream. Cover the cake with sliced strawberries or raspberries and curls of chocolate or chocolate decorations.

You can also make a delicious chocolate version by replacing 50 g of the self-raising flour with 50 g of cocoa powder.

MINI PIZZAS This recipe makes the base for 10 mini pizza rounds. Preheat the oven to 230ºC. Sift 350 g of plain flour, 2 tsp of easy-blend dried yeast and 2 tsp of salt into a bowl. Add 2 tbsp of olive oil, mix in and gradually add 250 ml of warm water until you have a soft pliable dough that does not stick to the bowl. Cover the bowl with clingfilm and allow to rise in a warm part of the kitchen for approximately 1 hour.

After the dough has nearly doubled in size, knock it back to get all the air out and knead it on a floured surface. Shape and roll into the pizza base sizes you require – I usually make them about 8 cm in diameter. Top with anything you like. For a fresh and simple choice, I use chopped fresh tomatoes, mozzarella and chopped basil. Another children's favourite is to mix tuna fish with lemon juice and a little crème fraîche and top it with a medium-strength cheddar and chopped chives to bring out the flavours. A more sophisticated pizza topping can be made by frying mushrooms and crispy bacon with garlic. Bake until the crust is golden brown, usually 10 minutes.

free your spirit at a
picnic lunch

SIMON SAYS... A picnic in a rural environment, far away from your home, will make it easier for you to feel relaxed and distanced from your normal life. Having a picnic in a park in an urban area will have a more yang chi energy than the countryside, and consequently may not be as relaxing, although parks often have the advantage of plenty of flowers and bright colours to enjoy. Parks are also more likely to have other people, making them social places. If you're planning a day out, the morning, with the sun rising in the sky, is an ideal time for games and activities, whereas the afternoon is better for relaxing, reading or having a nap.

The weather can make or break a picnic. Strong sunshine is yang, bringing energy, enthusiasm and high spirits – but make sure you don't burn your skin. Windy conditions are yang, clearing the mind and bringing new ideas. Clouds and rain are yin, calming emotions and making the mood more intimate. Snow is the most yin of weather conditions. A thunderstorm brings powerful yang chi energy.

THE IDEAL PICNIC SPOT

The type of natural environment or landscape that you choose for your picnic will influence the way that you feel – so be sure to pick a location that suits the occasion.

A mountain setting has a strong flow of chi energy moving vertically, providing a stimulating yang environment. It is ideal if you want to get in touch with your independent, spiritual or creative side. The higher and rockier the terrain, the more quickly chi energy will flow and the more yang and stimulating your picnic will become.

Flat lowlands have a greater flow of horizontal chi energy. This helps to carry chi energy from one person to the next, making them good locations for social events, such as gatherings, parties and intimate picnics for two. The chi energy of the plants, trees and grasses encourage these picnic spots to be more yin.

Fresh, unpolluted water can revive your energy levels and promote good health, and many people seek out the sea and natural spas to recuperate or convalesce. Sea water is more yang than fresh water, and bathing in natural salt water activates the chi energy of the salty fluids inside your body, making you more energised. If you're after a relaxing day, seek out a beach where the sea is calm, or if you want something more invigorating, choose high waves.

Rivers and moving water in general provide a good source of positive chi energy. Ideally, situate yourself on the inside of a bend in the river so that the water flows towards and then around you. A fast-flowing river is more yang and dynamic, whereas a slow river helps to calm your chi energy.

Lakes and other areas of still water are yin, producing a tranquil and relaxing chi energy. This still chi will make you feel peaceful and thoughtful, although make sure it is not polluted, which can have a negative effect on your chi.

WHEN YOU EAT OUTSIDE, YOUR OWN CHI ENERGY FIELD ABSORBS THE NATURAL AMBIENT CHI, HELPING YOU FEEL RELAXED, REFRESHED AND REVITALISED. PICK YOUR PERFECT PICNIC SPOT ACCORDING TO THE MOOD YOU WANT TO CREATE.

STEVEN SAYS... Whether you plan to cater for a day at the races with a group of colleagues or an afternoon boating with your loved one, a picnic is an excellent opportunity to show off your home cooking. It can be as grand or as simple as you wish, but do go to the trouble of supplying proper cutlery, crockery, linen and glasses, which all add a special feeling of decadence. Load a hamper with as many extravagant foods as you can and wash it all down with Champagne – you will be talked about for ever.

Picnics to me present perfect dip situations, with a range of prawns, bread and vegetables for dunking. Try my spicy shoyu dip (see page 77), or the tangy voodoo salsa (see page 151), or a hearty dollop of hummus (see page 121). Cut any fruit and vegetables into bite-sized chunks. More unusual dip-ables include baby corn, cherry tomatoes, courgettes, celeriac, fennel, radishes and even raw mooli if you want something a little peppery. My home-made bread recipes (see page 154–5) make great accompaniments.

My roasted vegetable bruschetta adds a lovely touch of refinement. Roast red peppers, red onions and cherry tomatoes in olive oil with plenty of fresh oregano and garlic and a little syrup. Chargrill a few slices of ciabatta bread, halve a garlic clove lengthways and rub the opened half over the bread. Then top each one lavishly with the vegetables and spoon over the oils.

Every picnic needs a few special treats, such as my juicy Dublin bay prawn skewers, which are easy to make and transport. Peel 6 cooked prawns and marinate them overnight in lemon oil (see page 153) with red chillies. Serve skewered on cocktail sticks, seasoned and sprinkled with a few roasted sesame seeds.

Sandwiches of some kind are also a must. Fresh bagels packed with smoked salmon, cream cheese and chopped chives are always popular – don't forget the freshly ground black pepper and squeeze of fresh lemon juice.

make your mark with a
housewarming party

SIMON SAYS... When you move into a new home, you will begin to make it your own with your own chi energy by introducing your furniture and decor to reflect your tastes and aspirations. Throw a housewarming party as well to help create a sense of belonging, as you fill the rooms with the convivial spirit and positive chi of your friends.

Before the party, however, you need to clear out the old chi energy of the previous occupants, which is best achieved by removing old fabrics, such as curtains, soft furnishings and perhaps

A NEW HOME IS THE PERFECT EXCUSE, IF EVER YOU NEED ONE, FOR A CELEBRATION. YOU ARE BOUND TO WANT TO SHOW OFF YOUR NEW PLACE TO YOUR FRIENDS AND FAMILY — AND A PARTY WILL ALSO HELP YOU TO ESTABLISH YOUR OWN CHI ENERGY THERE.

even the carpets. If you intend to keep any of them, wash them thoroughly. These types of materials tend to absorb chi energy over the years and could harbour chi generated by negative experiences in the past, such as arguments, tensions or bad feelings. The next step is to give the home a complete clean – wash the walls, floors and ceilings to refresh and renew the chi energy. Make sure that you clean the kitchen well as it is here that stale chi energy can upset your health and physical well-being.

To bring about an initial change in atmosphere, make your home more yang and get the chi energy moving faster, turning over the old energy.

Once you have cleaned out the old chi energy it is time to bring in new energy. One way to do this is to have a big party to celebrate moving in. All your friends and family will bring their own chi energy, helping you turn over the chi energy in the space; the more people you invite, the greater warmth they will generate. In addition, people feeling happy and enjoying a party will radiate a positive chi energy, as will loud music and dancing.

If you want to have a more wild party, it would be best to do this while the home is as empty as possible and the chi energy is free to move quickly. This makes a more powerful initial difference to the ambient chi energy of the space as it is better suited to people being more yang. Alternatively, wait until your home has been furnished and decorated and then have a more civilised or sophisticated house warming party.

After the party, have a good clear up to cleanse the chi energy. One further method to help clear the chi energy and remove the impurities when moving to a new home is to sprinkle sea salt on the floors before you go to bed at night. Sweep up or vacuum the floors the next morning and throw the salt away.

STEVEN SAYS... Fill your home with exotic smells to give your guests a warm welcome as they walk through the door. The best way to do this is to cook a spicy stew or even a curry dish. A vegetable broth packed with potatoes, carrots and flavoured with Indian spices is delicious served with warm home-made breads and pickles. Alternatively, you could make a vegetarian chilli like the spicy bean cassoulet (see page 57) with plenty of fresh red and green chillies. You can also warm your guests up with a hot punch, like Austrian Gluhwein – ideal for a cold winter's evening.

AUSTRIAN GLUHWEIN This recipe serves approximately 6, so multiply as necessary. Simply pour 1 litre of red wine into a saucepan and add 2 cinnamon sticks, 2 tbsp of honey, 1 orange studded with whole cloves, and the juice of 2 lemons and 2 oranges. Do not boil but warm gently for 15–20 minutes. Strain into a warm bowl and serve.

WARMING VEGETABLE BROTH This serves approximately 6 people, and the secret is to make it extra flavoursome with wine, garlic and spices. Use any vegetables for this – the more varied the ingredients, the better – up to a raw weight of about 2–3 kg. My basic selection includes: red onion, pumpkin, parsnip, celery, potatoes, swede, courgettes, baby corns, mushrooms, broccoli, cauliflower, mangetout and beans. Cut all the vegetables into approximately 4 cm chunks.

Heat a little olive oil in a large saucepan over a medium heat. Fry the onions for about 10 minutes. Add all the chopped vegetables, except those that don't need a long cook, such as beans, broccoli, cauliflower and mangetout. Add 2 cloves of crushed garlic and 1 red chilli, deseeded and finely sliced. Fry over a medium heat for a further 10 minutes, stirring continuously.

Add 1 litre of vegetable stock (see page 150), a glass of red wine and 2 tsp of garam masala (see page 149). Season to taste, stir well, cover and leave to simmer for 1 hour.

Add the remaining vegetables and 2 tbsp chopped fresh coriander and simmer for 10 minutes. Season again if necessary and serve immediately. You can also allow it to cool and keep it covered in the refrigerator for up to 4 days.

FILO PARCELS These are lovely, easy-to-make finger foods that look great and taste sensational. I like to fill mine with poached salmon and chives, but you can choose your own filling. My other favourites include dolcelatte with tomatoes and basil, fried bacon and mushrooms and tuna with sweetcorn and a little mayonnaise (particularly popular with children). Serve with dips if you like.

Preheat the oven to 230°C. Cut out 8 squares of filo pastry, approximately 15 cm x 15 cm. Brush melted butter on one side of each with a pastry brush. Fill with poached salmon (you will need about 150 g for 8 parcels) and chopped fresh chives and gather up edges to form a purse. Brush with melted butter and bake until golden, about 10 minutes.

THE FIERY CHI ENERGY OF A BARBECUE MIXED WITH THE FRESHNESS OF NATURE MAKES A PERFECT WAY TO BRING YOUR FRIENDS AND FAMILY TOGETHER IN A FUN, INFORMAL SETTING. THE FIRE ENCOURAGES PEOPLE TO BE OUTGOING AND EXPRESSIVE, AND BEING OUTSIDE PROMOTES A WONDERFUL FEELING OF FREEDOM.

fire up the atmosphere of a
barbecue

SIMON SAYS... If the weather is good, invite a few friends around and cook some food in the open air and on a natural flame. The food will absorb the fresh chi energy from nature, harmonising your personal energy with the world around you. The fresher the ingredients, the more powerful the chi, so pick home-grown vegetables just before cooking. In the same way, buy newly caught fish – or even catch your own – as close to the cooking time as possible.

The type of barbecue that you use will influence the character of the food you cook. A metal one will be the most yang and will contain and focus the heat. A brick or stone barbecue is more yin, and tends to diffuse the heat better. Build the bricks or stones into a three-sided oven and place a metal grate across the top. A hollow in the ground would be most yin, providing a gentle heat to prepare the foods. Dig a shallow hollow and burn the fire inside with a grate across the top.

When it comes to choosing the fuel, wood – and particularly wood ash – would be best for a light yin style of cooking. Charcoal burns at a higher temperature than wood, making this a yang heat source. The charcoal also retains its heat for longer, ideal if you are cooking for a lot of people.

STEVEN SAYS... Barbecues and al fresco parties in the open air are the highlights of my summer. I always have a huge barbecue and invite all my friends and family at least once a year. The real secret to a successful barbecue is the company – you can't go wrong among good friends having a good time. Providing them with great food is easy because that lovely barbecue flavour infuses everything you cook, and it all takes a small amount of time beforehand to prepare and organise your food.

Fish is ideal for a barbecue as it cooks well over a natural heat. To bake, coat with sesame, sunflower or olive oil and wrap in aluminium foil with fresh herbs and spices. Heat gently on glowing coal ashes. If you are cooking fish or meat, marinate it for a few hours before you cook to give it that extra depth of flavour. You can use these marinades for basting all kinds of food – including vegetables – as they sizzle on the barbecue. Below are the recipes for some of my favourite barbecue marinades.

BARBECUE SPICE MARINADE This marinade is good for both fish and meat, although it goes particularly well with chicken, duck and lamb fillets. Simply take a bowl and mix together the following ingredients: 2 tbsp of paprika, 4 deseeded and finely chopped red chillies, 1 tsp of ground cumin, 1 tsp of coriander seeds, 1 tsp of brown sugar, ½ tsp of dry mustard, 4 tbsp of tomato ketchup, 2 tbsp of olive oil and season well. Brush it thickly onto meat or fish and leave it covered in the fridge for a minimum of 2 hours before cooking.

SPICY SHOYU AND BLACK PEPPER MARINADE Ideal for red meat, this marinade also works well with oily fish like salmon, trout and sardines. Just mix together 200 ml of shoyu sauce, 100 ml of molasses (or honey), 3 tbsp of sesame oil, 1 tsp of Tabasco and 1 tbsp of black pepper. Brush on seconds before use (no need to marinate). Occasionally baste as you cook.

BARBECUED VEGETABLES I love serving vegetable kebabs because they are delicious and the barbecue brings out the vegetables' sweetness. I like to use wooden sticks or lemongrass skewered with bite-sized chunks of peppers, courgette, onion, cherry tomatoes, mushrooms and celery. You can add extra flavour with a bay leaf in the centre, but make sure that your guests don't eat it! Brush a marinades over the vegetables as they cook.

Big flat mushrooms are great barbecued on their own, as are asparagus spears and sweetcorn. Fennel and aubergines need to be sliced thinly and painted with olive oil before putting them on the barbecue. Corn on the cob can be chargrilled or buried in the ashes wrapped in foil. Chestnuts make perfect, warming barbecue food. Hold the chestnuts over the fire with a long fork or skewer until the outer skins start to crack open.

BARBECUED EXOTIC FRUITS SKEWERS These lovely exotic fruit skewers can be kept warm beside the barbecue, taking up more of that delicious barbecue flavour until they are served. You can use any sort of exotic fruit, including papaya, banana, star fruits, mangoes, pineapple, apricots and tamarillo, cut up into chunks of approximately 4 cm.

Prepare a sugar syrup dressing by very gently heating 50 g of raw cane sugar, 300 ml of water, 1 stick of cinnamon, 1 sprig of rosemary and the juice of 2 lemons until the sugar has completely dissolved. Simmer just below boiling point for 5 minutes, remove from heat and allow to cool for 5 minutes.

Next, place the fruit chunks in the sugar syrup dressing to soak for 5 minutes. Remove them and barbecue quickly on a hot flame to give them a marking and colour. Skewer the barbecued fruits and serve immediately with crème fraîche, thick natural yogurt or clotted cream.

STEVEN'S BARBECUE COCKTAIL This barbecue cocktail is a winner and really gets the party rolling! The secret is to keep it ice cold, especially on a hot summer afternoon. The method is simple: in a 2 litre jug, mix ½ litre of Absolut vodka citron (ice cold from the freezer), 1 litre of cranberry juice, 350 ml of good grapefruit juice (freshly squeezed and organic if possible), the juice of 6 limes and 3 oranges and 500 ml of sparkling mineral water. Throw in a couple of sliced fresh limes and plenty of ice, and drink it straight away or keep it chilled in the refrigerator until needed.

charge the energy at a
celebration party

SIMON SAYS... When you're planning a party, bear in mind that the timing is all-important, so pick your date carefully. At the time of a full moon, for example, people become more yang, making them outgoing and dynamic. If you want to throw an exciting and wild party, hold it a few days before the full moon – because everyone will be in a party mood. Take care, however, because accidents are more common at this time. If you prefer a more relaxed and harmonious party, fix a date around the new moon.

Fast-flowing chi energy encourages people to get up and dance, feel expressive and let their hair down. You can speed up the chi in the room with flashes of bright yang colours, such as red, yellow and purple, which make

CLEAR YOUR PARTY SPACE SO THAT CHI ENERGY CAN FLOW SWIFTLY AND FREELY BETWEEN YOUR GUESTS. FRESH, MOVING CHI ENCOURAGES BETTER EXPRESSION AND INTERACTION, BRINGING AN EXTRA BUZZ OF EXCITEMENT TO YOUR PARTY.

the atmosphere exciting. Decorate the room with bright lights, coloured flowers, streamers and balloons.

Mirrors are excellent for speeding chi energy flow and creating an exciting atmosphere. They also can make the room feel larger, giving the illusion that there is more space to move. The shiny, reflective surfaces of metallic mobiles or mirrored balls spin the energy around the room quickly, adding a feeling of exhilaration. If you are holding a party during the day, hang a crystal near a window to bring chi energy from outside in to your home – if you leave the window open, a breeze may spin the crystal to increase this flow of chi.

Yang foods, including salty and dry foods (see page 13), encourage people to be more active and outgoing and to dance more. Avoid providing too many yang snacks, though, as these can produce a craving for water and other yin liquids, including alcoholic drinks. Serve savoury food early in the proceedings and save yin desserts or cakes until the party is well under way; if people eat desserts early, they will be less active.

In a new year's party, the crucial moment is the changing of the year at midnight. A large clock, or several clocks, help to establish the appropriate atmosphere and serve as a constant reminder of the excitement of the new year. Mark the turning of the year by ringing a hand bell, which refreshes and renews the chi energy. Outdoor fireworks can have a similar effect.

STEVEN SAYS... I love the excitement of throwing a party – the rushing around clearing up and preparing food beforehand and that wonderful moment when you're surrounded by friends and family, feeling that warm, tingling pleasure inside. We open our house every New Year's Eve for a grand knees-up with singing and dancing and general indulgence. I prepare snacks and a finger buffet – snippets of big tastes and exotic flavours to add a frivolous feel that helps the party spirit. Throw in a huge bowl of punch, drink up and enjoy yourselves.

For the finger buffet, I like to have some tasty seafood with dipping sauces. The vermicelli king prawns with green chilli sauce (see page 114) are ideal, or try the king prawn tempura with shoyu dressing (see page 77). You can make tasty onion bhaji (see page 113), marlin brochettes (see page 102), sushi (see page 80) or fill wonton rolls with anything you like (see page 40).

I always like to deep fry my own crisps in very hot oil (275°C). The knack is to plunge them into the hot oil for 3 minutes, remove and salt them while they're still piping hot. You can also add some spice – curry powder, nutmeg or chilli powder all work well. In the winter, I often roast almonds in an oven heated to 200°C. Sprinkle them with sugar and salt and serve them while they're still warm.

A great party food, garlic bread is simple to make and you can leave it next to the oven for when you need it. Slice a French stick vertically, but not totally through the stick, and fill each pocket with a mixture of soft butter, fresh garlic, herbs and a little salt. Wrap it in tin foil and bake in the oven for 15 minutes.

CROSTINI WITH TOMATO, DOLCELATTE AND BASIL Preheat the oven to 180°C. Cut a French stick into approximately 12 slices, about 2 cm thick, and lay them flat on a lightly oiled baking tray. Drizzle extra virgin olive oil over them and rub in a small quantity of crushed garlic (2 cloves per loaf). Bake in the oven for about 10 minutes until golden and crisp. Remove from the oven and place a thin slice of beef tomato on top of each slice. Top the slices of tomato with approximately ½ tablespoon of dolcelatte and put it back into the oven for a few minutes to melt the cheese. Serve each crostini topped with chopped fresh basil.

For those who prefer life without blue cheese, try a strong goat's cheese. Other alternative toppings include some aubergine and garlic dip or tapenade (see page 121).

STEVEN'S PARTY COCKTAIL My notorious punch is always a success and makes about 3 litres. Mix 6 tbsp of brandy with 4 tbsp of caster sugar and leave to macerate for 1 hour. Stir in the juice of 2 lemons and 2 oranges, and add 2 tbsp of Curaçao or Grand Marnier. Now add 2 bottles of good Claret, stir and chill well. Just before serving, add 500 ml of sparkling water, ice and sliced lemon.

invite auspicious chi to a
wedding celebration

SIMON SAYS... The way in which a marriage begins has a great impact on the long-term success of the relationship. So it is vital on the day of the wedding not only to get the right balance of dignity, romance and celebration, but also to ensure that the chi energy is positive and appropriate for the occasion. It is also a celebration of the beginning of a romance and life-long friendship and therefore it also should have a festive and happy atmosphere.

Part of the ritual of the wedding is to bring friends and relations together to witness a public declaration of love and commitment between two people. It is important that this aspect of marriage is recognised and treated with respect. Remember that the chi energy of those witnessing the marriage ceremony will influence the energy of the couple and how they feel about the vows they are taking; make sure that you are in a positive mood and have the right chi energy.

The venue for the marriage ceremony itself will influence the flow of chi. A religious building, for example a church, mosque, synagogue or temple, will have a solid, well-established atmosphere that can add gravity or a sense of ceremony. The chi energy of worship will have become part of the building, and this will subtly affect the couple and the guests. Whether the wedding is a religious or a civil one, an older

A WEDDING HAS A SPECIAL SIGNIFICANCE AS IT MARKS THE BEGINNING OF A MARRIAGE, AND THE POSITIVE, HEALTHY ENERGY GENERATED AT A WEDDING CELEBRATION WILL REMAIN WITH THE COUPLE FOR THE WHOLE OF THEIR MARRIED LIVES.

building will have a greater presence of historic chi energy, endowing the ceremony with a more formal atmosphere. A wedding in a relatively new building, on the other hand, will have fresh chi energy, which is helpful if you see the event as making a new start.

Outdoor weddings at a beach or in a meadow, have open and relaxed atmospheres, encapsulating a sense of freedom. Much depends on the weather, which has its own powerful chi energy (see page 126).

The location of the reception depends on how many guests you are inviting. If you want the whole event to have an air of dignity, organise the reception in a grand, old building, making the atmosphere more formal and yang. Choose food to match (see pages 68–73 for setting menus for a formal occasion).

Having the reception at home, perhaps with a marquee in the garden, will bring the wedding symbolically into the family. This can make it a more intimate, friendly occasion, especially if you want it to be a family-orientated wedding with lots of children. A marquee will have a more temporary atmosphere, although it does bring in chi energy direct from nature. If the reception is in the garden, there is a risk that people will disperse too much and the event can lose its focus, making the party overly yin and lacking in sparkle and excitement. You can counter this by erecting a subtle boundary to keep the guests from straying.

STEVEN SAYS... The most special day of most peoples' lives, a wedding needs to be perfect in every way – including the food. Both of my restaurants have big weddings every year and we like to treat each one differently, getting to know the couple and their family and what they require. Good food is essential and I always like to provide canapés to add that air of extravagance and celebration. If you follow with a sit-down meal, you'll have a formal atmosphere. A buffet, on the other hand, allows people to move around and socialise, providing an exciting buzz. I love the decadent platters of seafood and other delicacies that you find on wedding buffets, and here are some of my favourites.

Pickled herring, shallot and sour cream canapés can be made by mincing pickled herring with chopped shallot, dill and seasoning. Spread the mixture onto warm toasted ciabatta and serve with a dollop of sour cream.

Lobster and truffle tartlets are made by placing a chunky piece of lobster tail in a tiny tartlet case. Add a disc of black truffle on top and a squeeze of lemon. Angels on horseback are made by rolling an oyster in bacon and fixing with a cocktail stick. Fry until bacon is cooked, and serve with a squeeze of lime.

Vine tomatoes with fluffy white crab can be prepared by blanching the tomatoes and removing the skin and the innermost flesh. Fill with fresh crab moistened with fresh lime, fresh crushed ginger, a little crème fraîche and seasoning.

BRING THE FAMILY TOGETHER IN AN ATMOSPHERE OF WARMTH AND JOY BY DECORATING YOUR HOME WITH FESTIVE LIGHTS AND ORNAMENTS. YOUR CHRISTMAS MEAL CAN BE MADE MORE EXCITING BY USING POLISHED CUTLERY, SHINY SILVER DISHES AND GLASSES ON THE TABLE. RED OR BRIGHT PURPLE NAPKINS AND FLOWERS WILL MAKE THE ATMOSPHERE MORE EXCITING. IF YOU WISH TO CREATE A MORE PEACEFUL ATMOSPHERE, USE GREEN NAPKINS, A CREAM TABLECLOTH AND WHITE FLOWERS.

capture the magic at
christmas

SIMON SAYS... The key to decorating for Christmas is balancing the yin and yang energy in the items you choose. For every yang decoration, match it with a yin one.

Gold, silver, purple and red decorations increase the exciting yang energy, especially if the objects are reflective and round, such as the shiny baubles on a Christmas tree. If the room is small, use fewer decorations or those with a matt finish to avoid over-charging the chi energy. Match these with yin, flowing fabrics, such as ribbons or soft furnishings with flowery

garlands in creams, pale greens and pale blues, to preserve warmth and harmony. Too many bright yang decorations make the home too stimulating, increasing the risk of tension; too few can stagnate the atmosphere, leading to disappointment.

Christmas trees have a spiky yang shape, which activate and stimulate a room's atmosphere. If you want the effect to be relaxing, use fabric tree decorations in neutral colours, such as cream-coloured bows, or straw or wooden ornaments. When choosing the size of the tree, try to keep it in proportion to the size of your room.

Too large a tree will dominate a small room, overwhelming the space and making it harder to relax. The ideal position for a Christmas tree would be to the north, east, south-east or south of a room. The five element energies of these directions – water, tree, tree and fire respectively – would be the most compatible with the energy of a Christmas tree.

Candlelight or fairy lights add a positive energy for Christmas, casting an intimate, warm and magical light on the proceedings. Make sure that you use candles safely; candles that clip onto your Christmas tree should be used with care.

In general, people are more likely to feel irritable and argue with each other when they feel claustrophobic and cooped up. You can help to relieve this by creating as much empty space as possible. When appropriate, get everyone to help you clear up, open the windows and refresh the atmosphere. If things seem to be getting tense, encourage everyone to go outside for a walk.

CHRISTMAS MEAL

Arrange the chairs so that people are seated in a circle or oval, if possible around a round-edged table. In particular, avoid seating anyone in the path of the fast-flowing, swirling energy close to a protruding corner – it could make that person feel on edge. Otherwise, seat people according to their personality, using the information on page 67. Those who are likely to be loud or excitable, for example, should face north so that they can absorb the calm and peaceful energy of this direction. The quieter or more shy guests can be seated facing south to encourage them to engage in conversation.

A diet rich in fats and added sugar strains and irritates the gallbladder, so you can adapt the traditional Christmas meal to prevent people feeling short-tempered or tired an hour or two after eating. First, include plenty of vegetables to help improve the balance of the meal. Second, help to break down the fats with radishes, vinegar, lemon and natural pickles. Third, avoid adding refined sugar to desserts. And lastly, don't overdo the Christmas toasts – too much alcohol overstimulates your liver.

STEVEN SAYS... Christmas is celebrated in many different ways across the world; the British love poultry, the French celebrate with lots of fresh seafood, and the Italians delight in panettone – a cake-like bread with dried fruit. I love goose or another form of poultry with all the trimmings on Christmas Day – it's often the only traditional meal I have all year round. A Feng Shui Christmas, however, is undoubtably going to be a healthy affair, and Simon admits that he likes to share a whole poached salmon with his family on Christmas Day.

It is easy to prepare a whole salmon if you have a large fish kettle. Simply cover the fish in the kettle with cold water, and add salt, peppercorns, some slices of lemon and a bouquet garni.

Bring the salmon to the boil on a medium heat (approximately 5–10 minutes depending on the size of the fish) and then immediately turn the heat off. Leave the fish in the kettle until the water is completely cool (approximately 2 hours) and the salmon will be cooked perfectly. Decorate with cucumber slices and serve with a yoghurt dip finished with lemon juice and coriander.

If there aren't enough of you for a whole salmon, you can buy a few chunky salmon fillets and pan fry them in olive oil with a little crushed garlic. Cook over a medium heat for 5 minutes on each side. Squeeze the juice of a lime over each one just before they are done. Serve on a bed of spinach with a dill, lemon and crème fraîche sauce.

eating out 5

When you eat out, you don't have as much control over the flow of chi energy as you do at home when you do the catering yourself, so it is especially important to pick the right restaurant for the occasion. The decor, layout and location of a restaurant, together with the type of food it serves and the chi energy and the people who work there, will all affect your personal chi and the way that you feel. So the kind of restaurant that suits a meeting with an important client is unlikely to work as well for a date or a boisterous family lunch. The next few pages show you how to ensure that you experience the ideal meal out.

choosing the right
restaurant

THERE'S AN ART TO SELECTING A
RESTAURANT: YOU NEED TO FIND A PLACE
THAT PROVIDES THE MOST APPROPRIATE
CHI ENERGY FOR THE OCCASION. TO CATCH
UP WITH AN OLD FRIEND, FOR EXAMPLE,
CHOOSE SOMEWHERE WITH A RELAXED,
YIN ATMOSPHERE WHERE YOU CAN TAKE
YOUR TIME AND CHAT WITHOUT BEING
DISTRACTED. HERE'S HOW TO MAKE
EVERY MEAL A SUCCESS...

SIMON SAYS... To help you decide where to book a table, you first need to think about the sort of chi energy you require. This will depend on the type of occasion, the number of diners, and the time of day you are planning to eat. You next need to consider the general type of restaurant that will provide the right kind of chi energy. This will depend on the restaurant's size, location, furnishings, food and clientele. Then all that remains is to pick a restaurant that fulfills your brief! Here are some tips for choosing the best type of restaurant for a range of occasions.

A grand celebration dinner with a group of people usually requires a formal restaurant. Opt for a prestigious country hotel with silver service and a first-class wine list, or a smart city restaurant with an excellent reputation. An old or historic building adds a solid chi energy, giving you a sense of tradition and grandeur, especially if the restaurant has been well-established for many years. Other details to look out for include the use of precious metals, especially silver and gold candlesticks, tableware, cutlery and so on, which increase the metal chi energy of the restaurant, making it more formal and prestigious. Crystal chandeliers spin chi energy around the room faster and can bring more exciting, fresh energy to a room, as can mirrors, especially those with ornate frames. High-ceilinged restaurants have more vertically moving chi energy, ideal for big ideas and far-reaching conversations, for avoiding sentimentality and keeping the atmosphere more auspicious and ceremonial.

A special celebration for two, such as an anniversary, may be better suited to a more intimate restaurant. A cosy country restaurant would create the perfect yin setting, ideally with plenty of soft furnishings to slow the pace of chi energy, making you feel more relaxed and able to unwind. Pastel yin colours, such as pink, pale green, pale blue and cream, add to the relaxing yin atmosphere. A low ceiling would be helpful for horizontally moving chi energy, which carries ideas, thoughts and feelings from one person to another, helping with mutual understanding and more emotional conversations.

For business you need a blend of sharp, confident yang energy with the ease and comfort of yin energy to keep you calm and relaxed. Modern designer restaurants can create the perfect ambience for entertaining, offering both contemporary and traditional dishes of beautifully prepared food in a crisply designed setting. The decor should match plenty of clean, shiny or metal yang surfaces with relaxed yin soft furnishings and calming shades. Increasin numbers of modern restaurants are using Feng Shui principles to provide the optimum atmosphere for eating. The result is that you feel confident, intellectual and expressive.

A meal out with friends provides an excellent way to get together, catch up and have fun. Help the evening along by choosing a busy restaurant with plenty of dynamic yang energy. A great idea would be to share sizzling dishes at a Chinese restaurant, placing them all on a spinning lazy Susan tray in the centre of the table to increase the movement of energy.

A COSY RESTAURANT WITH LOW CEILINGS IS IDEAL FOR A QUIET DINNER FOR TWO. CHOOSE A COUNTRY RESTAURANT IF YOU WANT MORE RELAXING YIN CHI ENERGY.

Alternatively, enjoy a dinner with live entertainment, where the sound will activate the ambient chi energy. A crowded restaurant can make you feel more social and interactive as other people radiate this type of chi energy.

Quick meals require a different kind of restaurant. Snack bars, cafés and fast-food chains provide a wealth of choice for a quick bite. Fast-food burger bars have highly yang atmospheres, speeding chi energy around quickly with bright lights, bright colours and shiny surfaces. They are designed to encourage you on your

A DYNAMIC YANG SPACE WITH HIGH CEILINGS AND PLENTY OF LIGHT MAKES THE ENVIRONMENT ENERGETIC AND VIBRANT FOR A FUN AND EXCITING NIGHT OUT.

BREAKFAST TAKES PLACE at the time of day associated with tree energy, which would favour a place that has tall ceilings, sunshine and plenty of the greenery – plants and flowers are a great way to refresh the chi energy. A table on a terrace or in a garden would provide a more inspirational chi energy. Breakfast is an ideal time to make plans for the day or set out the agenda for new projects. Exposure to the rising sun in the east would provide plenty of positive chi energy for the morning, so choose an east-facing café or sit facing eastwards at the breakfast table.

BREAKFAST

way and to clear the space for new customers. Many people find these areas too yang to enjoy their food and prefer the more relaxed atmosphere of a snack bar, diner or café. Most places that fall into this category are slightly less clinical and yang, providing more comfortable and friendly surroundings for you to enjoy a quick meal and rest for a few minutes before leaving.

Japanese noodle and sushi bars are often yang spaces, matching the trimly presented food with minimalist decor, speedy service and a quick customer turnover. The swift yang energy makes them excellent places for increasing your energy.

Finding the right restaurant for a family meal with children can make all the difference between a relaxing meal and one that is fraught with tension. Children often respond quickly to different environments, so it is worth experimenting. A less crowded place with high ceilings and more open space would be a good starting place. Children love to be occupied and stimulated, so a restaurant with plenty of activities, games and things to look at can keep them happy. Some places have play areas or provide colouring-in place mats or puzzle sheets. Other useful distractions are water features, aquariums and moving objects, such as mobiles or windchimes. A restaurant with plenty of plants will often have a more soothing atmosphere which can help to calm over-excited children.

THE AMBIENCE AND NOISE

The atmosphere of the restaurant and the way your meal develops will be affected by the other diners. Restaurants tend to attract a particular type of clientele. A lively brasserie with modern dishes and design will pull a young, fashionable crowd, while a classic restaurant with a refined environment will be more popular

LUNCH IS ASSOCIATED with the midday fire chi energy, and suits a location with plenty of natural light, bright colours and lively staff. A lunch with colleagues or friends should be friendly and buzzing with laughter and good conversation. Lunch with a client requires a bright, crisp atmosphere and efficient service to present the right impression. High ceilings and plenty of glass help to keep the conversation fast, friendly and less personal. However, if you want to have a relaxing lunch to get to know someone better, you may prefer a more comfortable yin atmosphere with soft furnishings.

LUNCH

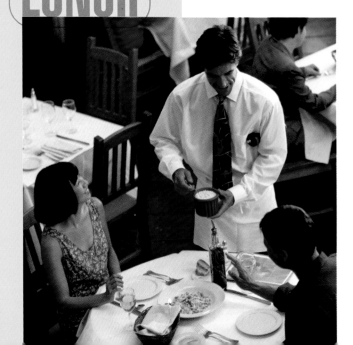

with older people. It is important that you feel comfortable when you are out. If you can, find out the type of clientele that frequent your chosen restaurant; you don't want to take your business client to a restaurant filled with romantic couples!

Music and background noise can have an enormous effect on the ambience of a restaurant. Gentle music can put you at ease, but be aware that places that play music very loud or with heavy beats make the atmosphere very yang; this can upset your digestion and distract you from your enjoyment of the meal. If the restaurant has a lot of background noise, you may find yourself shouting to be heard; but if the place is quiet enough to hear a pin drop, you may feel too self-conscious to have a private conversation.

It can also be difficult to talk openly if the tables are too close together. According to Feng Shui, soft music or the sound of running water can be used to help prevent chatter from spoiling your meal and fellow diners from overhearing your conversation.

THE SERVICE

The staff that serve you have a great impact on the way you feel and react to your surroundings. A friendly, relaxed and chatty service is great if you are out for fun with friends, but may be unhelpful if you are having an intimate dinner for two and want to concentrate on each other. Silver service is perfect for a formal occasion, although it can be too austere for some. As a general rule, fast, yang staff quicken your pace of eating, and a slow, yin service is preferable if you want to feel more relaxed.

IF YOU ARE GOING OUT WITH FRIENDS before the theatre or prior to another form of entertainment, you will want somewhere quick and informal, such as a lively bistro or brasserie. Bright lights, large windows and minimal soft furnishings speed the flow of chi

EARLY DINNER

energy, encouraging everyone to feel animated and excited. Natural wood provides tree chi energy, good for growth and quick thinking which can improve your concentration for the evening ahead. If the tables are laid out in formal lines, the atmosphere will help you stay alert and ready for action.

LATE-NIGHT SUPPER

A RELAXED SUPPER after an evening out is a perfect opportunity for an intimate dinner for two. Night-time is associated with water chi, helping you to feel affectionate and calm. Choose a cosy yin restaurant with low ceilings that will help socialising and mutual understanding. Low table lighting or candles, comfortable seating and an imaginative yin layout all help slow the pace and provide an intimate ambience. A basement restaurant or one with alcoves produces an enclosed, private atmosphere, conducive to feeling less inhibited and more open with your feelings.

THE LOCATION

Every restaurant will have different chi energy according to its location and the surrounding area. Chi energy flows quickly down busy main roads, for example, and this will speed the chi energy within a restaurant on the road, making it more yang. If the restaurant is situated with a road coming towards it – at the head of a T-junction or at the centre of a fork, for example – it will have a rush of chi energy that may make it too yang for healthy eating. Restaurants that are located next to large junctions and

SIT OUTSIDE A RESTAURANT IF YOU WANT NATURAL CHI ENERGY THAT HELPS YOU FEEL CLOSER TO NATURE AND ENHANCES FREE THINKING. STAY INSIDE IF YOU WANT A MORE COSY YIN ENERGY, ALLOWING YOU TO HAVE DEEPER, MORE INTIMATE CONVERSATIONS.

roundabouts may have a similar problem. You should also be careful if a restaurant has the corner of another large building pointing towards it; this will result in cutting chi – a chaotic movement of chi energy that can make the atmosphere fraught, agitated and uncomfortable.

According to Feng Shui principles, a restaurant in a city will be a busier and more vital space with a yang atmosphere, whereas a country house restaurant has more yin energy with a slower, more relaxing pace. A cluster of similar yang restaurants in a city centre can make for low prices and good quality as each competes with its neighbours for customers. On the other hand, yin restaurants that are isolated often develop more innovative menus.

A restaurant on a river or next to the sea or a lake provides an excellent opportunity to improve your health and enhance your well-being with water chi energy. Fast-flowing water creates a yang environment with plenty of fresh chi to revitalise you. Still water on a lake will provide a more calming yin chi. You will feel the benefit of water energy far more if you eat in a boat restaurant. A beach restaurant will capture the atmosphere of the time of day, whether the hot sunshine of midday or the setting sun.

Choose a restaurant at the top of a tall building if you want to feel independent and objective. This type of setting is influenced by vertically moving energy, enabling you to feel detached and view the world from a different angle, providing a good opportunity to look back on your life, take stock and plan for the future. As such, these places are ideal for new year, anniversary or birthday celebrations.

A restaurant in a cellar or partially underground provides a more secure, comforting chi energy that can help if you feel uncertain or need solace. The chi energy moves slowly and horizontally, helping you to come to terms with your emotions and to express how you feel. However, the chi can become stagnant in some underground restaurants and you may find yourself becoming lethargic.

If you are eating in a garden or on a terrace, you will be taking on the chi energy of different weather conditions (see page 126) and the natural and more free chi energy of the outdoors. This may not be advantageous if you are in a group, however, as the free-moving chi energy may disperse people.

TABLEWARE

PROVIDING AN IDEAL MEANS FOR CREATING THE RIGHT AMBIENCE, tableware is a great tool for altering the yin or yang balance of a room. Thick, soft napkins and tablecloths in pastel colours slow the flow of chi energy, producing a more relaxing yin atmosphere. Paper tablecloths and serviettes increase the speed of chi and create a yang atmosphere with a fast turnover of customers.

COLOURS

A SPACE WITH BRIGHT YANG COLOURS, such as a fast-food restaurant, will have a great charge of fast-flowing energy that makes it difficult to feel relaxed. Clean, white walls also make the space yang because they reflect energy around the room.

Cream, pink, pale green and pale blue are yin colours, calming a space. Matt black is also yin as it absorbs the light and makes a room deficient in chi energy, allowing you to feel laid back and relaxed.

MATERIALS

PLENTY OF FLAT, shiny and hard surfaces, such as marble, stone and polished wood, encourage chi energy to move quickly, keeping the atmosphere alive and yang and promoting quick, lively discussions.

If the restaurant has more soft or rough-textured surfaces, such as carpets, rugs and matting, the chi within will be yin and contained. This will allow you to feel secure and better able to focus your attention on one subject.

LAYOUT

A RESTAURANT THAT HAS A regimented layout – arranged in straight lines – makes the space organised and yang. The waiting staff move along clearly defined energy paths and serve customers quickly. A yin layout would have tables arranged in irregular patterns, forcing people to meander.

LIGHTING

FOR A QUIET, YIN ATMOSPHERE, a restaurant with table lighting, preferably with candles, provides the ideal lighting. If you want a more dynamic yang environment, a space with direct halogen lighting creates a more forceful chi energy that can fire up your meal. White ceilings reflect all the light frequencies, and can magnify the effect of strong lighting creating a highly yang space. Soft-coloured walls reflect less light and are more yin.

selecting an appropriate
restaurant menu

STEVEN SAYS... The menu sells the restaurant; it doesn't matter how great the location or interior is, if the food is poor the restaurant will ultimately fail. But this does not necessarily mean that the menu must be creative or innovative, it just needs to include premium quality ingredients – fresh and seasonal. I need to know that the food I am preparing is of top quality – free from additives, genetically modified ingredients and other unnatural qualities – which means using organic or home-grown ingredients as much as possible.

There are now a number of restaurants that specialise in using natural ingredients to create balanced dishes. Many use only organic products, blending the full flavours to make often highly innovative, great-tasting dishes. Balancing the yin and yang aspects of food has become popular in many health-conscious restaurants, especially those that specialise in Eastern cuisine.

Working with nature also means working with the seasons. When I write a menu, I shut myself in my office, close my eyes and reflect on the time of year. The idea is to select foods at their optimum time and carefully cook them to bring out that special seasonal flavour. Spring is ideal for lamb, spring vegetables, the first asparagus, fresh herbs and a lightness and freshness to food. Summer marks the ripening of strawberries and cherries, the first peas in their pods, when tomatoes and crisp salads are all at their best. Autumn brings a harvest of apples and pears, plums and greengages, wild blackberries, corn on the cob, and the first root vegetables ready for roasting. Winter means warming stews, thick soups, game, chestnuts, hot spongy puddings, Christmas nuts and dried fruits. I look outside and try to impart a feeling of the season to create dishes that harmonise the internal body with the external environment.

SIMON SAYS... It is as important to find the right menu for an occasion as the right ambience. The food that you eat has a great influence on your chi energy and the success of the meal.

ITALIAN I go to an Italian restaurant for a lively fun evening, perhaps when I want to meet a group of friends for an active social occasion. The atmosphere tends to be colourful and fun, and the food blends healthy ingredients with great tastes.

JAPANESE
I find Japanese foods helpful for feeling mentally stimulated for clear thinking. They often make an effort to balance the chi energies in every meal.

CHINESE I find the powerful flavours and rich sauces provide plenty of fire energy, helpful if you want to be quick and active. Choose restaurants that do not use MSG and other additives.

THAI With exquisite flavours and ambience, I like to share Thai meals with interesting friends and have good conversation.

FRENCH Eating at a good French restaurant is usually a sensual delight, and I enjoy the more formal French cuisine for special occasions, such as birthday dinners or anniversary celebrations.

Each menu needs to take consideration of the type of clientele the restaurant attracts and what kind of eating experience they expect. An old country house restaurant that is popular for dinners for two requires a menu with soft, sumptuous dishes, such as steamed turbot, soufflé of Dover sole or poached wild salmon. The customers have come for the comfortable ambience and good reliable dishes of unwavering quality. My country cottage restaurant, The Pink Geranium,

THE DISHES ON THE MENU SHOULD REFLECT THE EXPECTATIONS OF THE CLIENTELE AND ALSO MATCH THE DESIGN AND AMBIENCE OF THE RESTAURANT.

needs a formal Cordon Bleu-style menu to bring a polished yet gentle tone to make each meal an occasion.

An upbeat brasserie, on the other hand, needs noisy, brash dishes, such as chargriddled sirloin, flash-seared squid or deep-fried prawns with spicy dips. My other restaurant, Sheene Mill, is a modern brasserie with the kitchens in full view of the restaurant and so I love to fill the menu with sizzling or flambé dishes and powerful aromas that waft into the dining area.

INDIAN Traditionally vegetarian, Indian cooking offers a wide variety of vegetable-based dishes that taste great and are good for your health. The food tends to be stimulating and can also make you feel more emotional and expressive.

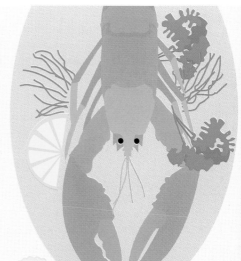

GREEK I get a warm feeling in Greek restaurants that have wonderful family atmospheres and go out of their way to make children feel welcome. Meze-style dishes are great for sharing and bringing the family together.

MACROBIOTIC The ultimate in healthy eating, I would expect all the ingredients to be organic and prepared with care. The meals are centred around a wide variety of grain, vegetable and bean dishes.

FISH The best fish restaurants are situated in seaside towns where the fish is extremely fresh. Seaside restaurants can help you to feel stronger, warmer and more yang.

appendix

WITH A GROWING RANGE OF INGREDIENTS available to us today, it is easy to feel confused or overwhelmed at the prospect of modern cooking. However, the key to creative cooking is to keep an open mind: don't be daunted about trying out new ideas. Some of the more unusual ingredients are featured below; most are available from large supermarkets, although you may need to go to speciality stores, such as Chinese or Japanese supermarkets, to find some of the ingredients.

Thai cookery would not be the same without lemongrass. I use it all the time for those distinct Thai flavours coupled with coconut milk, fresh chillies and coriander. The dried variety is no real substitute for fresh lemongrass. Cut it into small pieces or bruise the stem to release the flavours.

From the tropical rain forests of America comes the vanilla pod – the fruit of the climbing orchid. The vanilla pod is expensive but far better than vanilla flavouring – the seeds scatter through sauces and creams making them look and taste wonderful.

The stamens of the saffron crocus produce a subtle, enriching flavour. They are expensive – the best are grown in La Mancha in Spain – and work wonderfully in rich sauces.

The Eastern radish, mooli or daikon, is a large white vegetable with a sweet, fresh flavour. You can shred it into a salad or a stir-fry, or pickle it using the method opposite. If you can't find it, use ordinary radishes.

FLAVOURINGS

chinese five spice and Japanese seven spice

Five spice is my favourite spice mixture, made from star anise, cloves, fennel seed, cinnamon and Szechuan pepper. Seven spice is made of chilli, mustard seeds, nori seaweed, poppy seeds, sansho leaves, sesame seeds and mandarin peel. Use them liberally with poultry, fish and vegetarian dishes.

nori seaweed

Commonly used in Japanese cooking, sweet-salty nori seaweed is usually bought in sheets, often already toasted, and used to make sushi or chopped and sprinkled over a rice or noodle dish.

hoi sin sauce

This is a product made from soya purée, lemon juice, garlic, spices and vinegar. It is a ready-made sauce that is easy to obtain from large supermarkets.

garam masala

Meaning 'hot spices', garam masala is a blend of spices. You can make about 5 tbsp by grinding together the following ingredients:

3 tbsp cardamom seeds
3 x 2.5 cm pieces of cinnamon stick
1½ tsp cumin seeds
½ tbsp black peppercorns
½ tsp cloves
¼ of a nutmeg

wasabi

Fresh wasabi root is rare outside Japan, but you are sure to find wasabi powder or wasabi paste in tubes. It is a very pungent purée of Japanese horseradish, dyed green, and used to accompany sushi, tempura and many other dishes.

mirin

A Japanese rice wine, mirin adds a delicate sweetness to sauces and stocks.

thai fish sauce

Made from fish and seafood stock, this pungent and highly flavoured sauce is used in a similar way to shoyu sauce (see page 14).

GARNISHES AND PICKLES

crispy deep-fried vegetables and herb leaves

This garnish can add extra flavour and colour to a range of dishes, and can be a vegetable, such as carrot, leek, beetroot, celeriac or turnip, or a herb, such as basil, coriander, sage, thyme or rosemary. Finely shred the vegetables, allowing about 1 tbsp per serving, or loosen the herbs into sprigs or single leaves. Heat a pan of vegetable oil to 175ºC. Fry the shredded vegetables for approximately 30 seconds (until slightly coloured), or the herbs for about 5 seconds. Remove immediately and drain. Season with salt, pepper and ground ginger while hot so that the flavours get absorbed.

pickled jalapeño

This is a slightly hot chilli originally from Jalapeño in Mexico. Bring 100 ml of white wine, 100 ml of white wine vinegar and 50 ml of honey to the boil, add 2 cloves of garlic and allow to cool. Put

the mixture with 8 jalapeño chillies in an air-tight jar and leave for 48 hours. They can be stored chilled for up to 8 weeks.

pickled vegetables

My favourite vegetables for pickling include carrots, leeks, daikon and mushrooms, although you can pickle just about anything you want. Mix 100 ml of wine vinegar with 100 ml of white wine and 1 tbsp or rice syrup. Cut the vegetables (about 500 g) into the sizes and shapes that you need, place them in a saucepan and pour over the pickling juice. Bring to the boil over a medium heat, then remove from heat immediately, strain and chill.

clear vegetable stock

Ideal for adding fresh herby flavours, a good vegetable stock provides extra depth and character to sauces and casseroles. This recipe will make about 1¾ litres, and you can keep it for up to 4 days in the refrigerator in an air-tight container. You can also freeze it, but be sure to sieve it beforehand.

2 onions, roughly chopped
1 leek, roughly chopped
3 stalks of celery, roughly chopped
2 carrots, roughly chopped
2 lemons, unwaxed and sliced
1 bulb of garlic, cut in half
   horizontally
2 star anise
6 whole black peppercorns
approximately 1½ litres cold water
2 tbsp chopped fresh coriander
1 tbsp chopped fresh thyme
250 ml dry white wine
salt and freshly milled black pepper

Put all the vegetables, the lemon and the garlic in a saucepan over a medium heat with the star anise and peppercorns. Cover with cold water and bring to the boil. When boiling, add the coriander, thyme and wine, remove from the heat and allow to cool and store covered in a refrigerator. Pour stock through a fine sieve and season to taste before use.

miso stock

Simmer 1 tbsp of a chopped vegetable of your choice with a 5 cm strip of kombu or wakame seaweed (available from health food stores) in 1 litre of water for 20 minutes. Remove from heat and stir in 3 tsp of miso bean paste (also available from health food stores).

fish stock

A good fish stock is aromatic and full of flavour; the secret is to keep cooking time to a minimum. This recipe makes approximately 1 litre.

½ tbsp grape seed oil
1 onion, roughly chopped
1 leek, roughly chopped
4 stalks of celery, roughly chopped
½ bulb of garlic, cut in half
   horizontally
1 small fennel bulb, chopped
approximately 250 g fish bones or
   off-cuts, chopped
750 ml dry white wine
approximately 1½ litres of water
salt and white pepper
2 tbsp chopped herbs of your choice

Heat the oil in a deep saucepan over a low heat and cook the vegetables for 5 minutes. Add the chopped fish bones or off-cuts and stir in thoroughly. Now add the wine and enough cold water to cover the ingredients. Bring to the boil over a medium-high heat, and then immediately reduce heat and bring down to a simmer. Skim the surface of the stock from time to time to get rid of any surface oil and scum. Simmer for 25 minutes.

Remove from the heat and pass the mixture through muslin or a fine sieve into a clean saucepan. Return to a medium-high heat and boil until the stock has reduced by half to concentrate the flavours. Season to taste and add the chopped herbs.

To finish you can add a 2–3 tbsp double cream, or allow to cool slightly and add 2–3 tbsp crème fraîche or natural yoghurt.

chicken or game stock

This recipe makes approximately 1 litre.

3 kg chicken or mixed game
   bones, chopped
60 g honey
1 tbsp grape seed oil
4 carrots, peeled and chopped
2 onions, cut in half
4 stalks celery, chopped
1 bulb of garlic, cut in half
   horizontally
1 leek, chopped
approximately 500 g ripe tomatoes,
   roughly chopped
approximately 1½ litres of
   water
1 litre red wine
1 tbsp chopped fresh thyme
1 bay leaf
6 whole peppercorns
salt and freshly milled black pepper

Preheat the oven to 230°C and cover the raw bones with honey in a large baking or roasting tray. Roast until golden brown – approximately 30–40 minutes – turning occasionally. In a large saucepan, heat the oil over a low heat and gently cook the vegetables for 5 minutes. Add the tomatoes and enough water to cover the vegetables. Over a medium-high heat, bring this to the boil, then add the roasted bones and skim the surface. Reduce the heat to low and simmer until the stock has reduced by half (usually several hours).

Pass the stock through muslin or a fine sieve into a clean saucepan and place over a high heat. Add the red wine and reduce until the stock has reduced by half again. Taste and add the herbs and seasoning. Pour the stock into a clean container and store overnight or for at least 6 hours to cool.

When cold scrape off and discard any surface fat. Keep refrigerated in an air-tight container for up to 4 days or freeze for up to 6 months.

lobster bisque

This is a light creamy sauce made from the lobster or prawn shells, or you can make a similar sauce using crab shells. This recipe makes approximately 1 litre.

3 lobster carcasses or approximately
    400 g of shells
½ tbsp grape seed oil
2 leeks, roughly chopped
2 carrots, roughly chopped
4 stalks of celery, roughly chopped
1 medium onion, sliced
8 tomatoes, cut in quarters
½ bulb of garlic, cut in half
    horizontally

1 tbsp chopped fresh tarragon
1 tbsp chopped fresh basil
approximately 1½ litres of fish
    stock or water
½ litre of dry white wine
150 ml double cream to finish
    (optional)
salt and freshly milled black pepper

Roast the shells in an oven preheated 230°C oven until crisp and brittle, approximately 30–45 minutes. Heat the oil in a large saucepan over a low heat and fry the vegetables and tomatoes for 5 minutes. Add the herbs and enough water to cover them, bring to the boil, reduce the heat and simmer for 5 minutes. Add the lobster shells and white wine. Top up the saucepan with either water or fish stock to cover the ingredients and bring to the boil.

As soon as it boils, reduce the heat and simmer for 1–1½ hours. Pass through a fine sieve into a clean pan over a high heat and reduce the stock down by at least half. Whisk in the double cream. Reduce again until it coats the back of a spoon. Taste, season and serve.

watercress purée

This is a terrific garnish for soups and sauces. When required, spoon a little into the hot soup or sauce and whisk in vigorously at the last moment to add flavour and colour. Makes 40 g.

2–3 bunches of watercress
approximately 1 tsp water
salt and freshly milled black pepper

Blanch the watercress for 10 seconds in boiling water then refresh. Now blend the watercress in a food processor with the water. The purée should be thick enough to form a paste. Season and keep covered in the refrigerator.

voodoo salsa

This spicy but sweet chilli sauce is a delicious accompaniment to almost anything. First developed by Dean Fearing – a world-class chef in Dallas, Texas – I have adapted it to create a more subtle flavour. Makes about 400 ml.

1 tbsp sesame oil
4 red peppers, deseeded and chopped
2 onions, chopped
4 cloves garlic, peeled and chopped
4 red chillies, deseeded and chopped
1 mango, peeled and cut from
    the stone
4 ripe tomatoes, quartered
1 tbsp fresh root ginger, grated
100 ml rice wine vinegar
250 ml fresh orange juice
150 ml dry white wine
salt and freshly milled black pepper
fresh coriander to finish

Heat the oil in a large pan over a low heat and gently fry the peppers, onions, garlic and chillies for 5 minutes. Add the mango, tomatoes, ginger and vinegar and

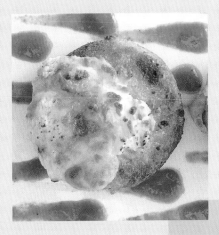

stir well. Now add the orange juice and wine and bring to the boil. Reduce the heat and simmer for 30–35 minutes. Pour into a blender and purée until smooth, then strain through a sieve.

Taste the salsa; you may need to add ½ tbsp of honey if the tomatoes are not sufficiently ripe.

Season to taste and add some chopped fresh coriander.

oven-dried tomatoes and tomato paste

You can't always rely on the sun to dry your tomatoes, so I use the oven instead. Once dried, you can make a strong, fresh tomato paste; purée the tomatoes and store in an air-tight container in the refrigerator.

12 ripe vine tomatoes
100 g sea salt or rock salt
4 cloves garlic, peeled and crushed
1 sprig of thyme
olive oil to preserve

Heat the oven to 140ºC. Halve or quarter the tomatoes and scatter the sea salt, garlic and thyme over a baking tray and then lay the pieces of tomato on top. Place in the oven for 1–1½ hours. The tomatoes should be dried, slightly chewy and a deep red colour. Brush off any salt and store covered in olive oil in an air-tight container.

orange and tomato coulis

This is a tangy, slightly spicy sauce that adds fresh flavours and colours. Use it with meat and seafood, it goes particularly well with chicken. This recipe makes about 400–500 ml – enough for 4 main course-meals – so

if you don't want that much, halve the quantities. Keep in an air-tight container in the refrigerator for up to 4 days.

1 tbsp olive oil
2 shallots, peeled and chopped
3 cloves garlic, peeled and crushed
150 ml white wine
1.8 kg tomatoes, cut into quarters
3 oranges, peeled and chopped
2 chillies, deseeded and finely sliced
salt and freshly milled black pepper

Heat the oil in a large saucepan over a low heat. Add the shallots and garlic and fry for 2 minutes, then add the wine, tomatoes, oranges and chillies. Bring to the boil, then turn the heat low, cover and simmer for 30 minutes. Remove the coulis from the heat, pour it into a liquidizer and purée. Pass it through a fine sieve into a jug, taste and season.

old-fashioned custard

This recipe serves 4 or makes 500 ml.

6 egg yolks
100 g caster sugar
1 vanilla pod
225 ml double cream
225 ml milk
1 tbsp cornflour
1 tsp cold water

Whisk the egg yolks with the sugar in a deep bowl until creamy. Split the vanilla pod in half and place it in a saucepan with the cream and milk. Slowly bring to the boil over a low heat and then pour it over the egg yolk mixture and whisk in thoroughly. In a small bowl or cup, mix the cornflour with the cold water and then add it to the custard. Whisk in well. Return the custard to a low heat and stir (or whisk) until thick and creamy.

sugar stock syrup

This is used for poaching fruit or for diluting a coulis, and also can be used as a base for a soufflé. This recipe makes approximately 300 ml.

75 g unrefined sugar or 1 tbsp maize syrup
300 ml water
1 vanilla pod
1 cinnamon stick
1 sprig of rosemary
zest from 1 unwaxed lemon, cut into large pieces
2½ cm piece of fresh root ginger, peeled and thinly sliced
2 pieces star anise

Put the sugar or syrup and water in a saucepan over a medium-high heat and bring to the boil. Add one or two of the flavourings above, but not more than two. I try to match good combinations, such as lemon and rosemary or cinnamon and vanilla pod.

Simmer for 3–5 minutes then add your fruits for poaching, or remove from heat, leave to cool and keep refrigerated in an air-tight container for up to 8 days for later use. If you freeze the syrup, remove any solid flavourings beforehand.

OILS AND DRESSINGS

Flavoured oils and dressings add rich colours and flavours to a dish. They are easy to make and can be kept in bottles (with a screw lid) in the refrigerator for up to a week without losing much colour; after that the colours will start to deteriorate but the flavours will remain the same for up to 2 months.

coriander or basil oil

Follow the same process for any green herb, such as tarragon, dill or mint.

1 large bunch (about 200 g) coriander or basil, including stalks
300 ml light olive oil or grape seed oil
salt and freshly milled black pepper

Remove any dead leaves and wash the herbs. Blanch them in boiling water for 5 seconds, then remove immediately and refresh in cold water. Squeeze out the water and put them into a liquidizer. Blend, adding the olive oil in two batches. Continue to blend for at least 2 minutes to ensure that all the colour and flavour is extracted.

Pour into a fine sieve lined with muslin and squeeze or press out the liquid into a clean bowl. Taste the oil, season and pour into bottles.

red pimento oil

3 red peppers
2 cloves garlic, peeled
750 ml light olive oil
a squeeze of fresh lemon juice

Preheat the oven to 200°C. Cut the peppers in half and discard the seeds, put the halves into a roasting tray with

the cloves of garlic and submerge with the oil. Put them into the oven for 30 minutes. Remove the peppers and garlic from the oil and blend in a food processor or liquidizer until smooth. Pass through a fine sieve into a clean bowl and set aside to cool. Separately, strain the cooking oil through a fine sieve and set aside to cool.

When the oil and peppers are cool, blend together with a squeeze of fresh lemon juice and whisk briskly to prevent the oil from emulsifying like mayonnaise!

lemon oil

This tasty oil can be made with limes.

300 ml light olive oil
zest and juice of 6 unwaxed lemons
salt and freshly milled black pepper

Put all ingredients in the food processor and blend for 2–3 minutes, then pour through a funnel into bottles. Allow to infuse for 24 hours for best results, then pass through a sieve lined with muslin to remove the lemon rind. Taste and season. Shake well before serving.

garlic oil

2 bulbs of garlic, unpeeled
1 sprig of thyme
100 ml olive oil
300 ml of grape seed oil to finish
sea salt

Preheat the oven to 200°C. Break the garlic cloves away from the bulbs, but do not peel them. Place them in a square of tin foil with the thyme and cover with 2 tbsp of olive oil. Fold over the tin foil

to make a little parcel, and then fold over the edges to seal. Bake in the oven for approximately 45 minutes or until the garlic is very soft inside the foil parcel.

Remove, cool and squeeze out the garlic from each clove. Put it into a food processor or liquidizer, cover with the remaining oil and blend for 3–4 minutes. Allow to stand for an hour to infuse the flavours, then taste and season. Pass through a muslin-lined sieve and chill.

horseradish oil

This is a delicious, pungent oil that is great with vegetables and salads. If you can't find fresh horseradish, use the bottled creamed variety.

200 ml freshly grated horseradish
200 ml grape seed oil
1 tbsp rice wine vinegar
salt and freshly milled black pepper

Put the horseradish and oil in a food processor and blend for 2–3 minutes. Add the vinegar, taste and season. Pass through a fine sieve, pour into bottles and chill for a few hours to infuse the flavours.

BREADS

Breads can be made more exciting by adding oven-dried tomatoes, olives, walnuts, sunflower seeds, raisins, or herbs such as coriander, thyme, rosemary and basil. Added ingredients alter the consistency, so you may have to add more flour or water if the dough becomes too dry or too wet.

farmhouse white crusty loaf

This recipe makes 1 large loaf or about 15–20 rolls, depending on size.

800 g strong flour
1 heaped tsp easy-blend dried yeast
1 tbsp salt
1 tsp unrefined or raw cane sugar
450 ml warm water

Butter a 900 g loaf tin and preheat the oven to 230ºC. Sift the flour into a bowl and add the yeast, salt and sugar. Make a well in the centre and add the water. Mix together with a wooden spoon and then knead the dough until elastic in texture. Cover the bowl with clingfilm and allow the dough to rest in a warm part of the kitchen until it has doubled in size, usually 1½–2 hours. Knead the dough for a few minutes to remove any air pockets. Put the dough into the buttered loaf tin and sprinkle the top with white flour. Allow to rest for half an hour to increase in volume.

Bake in the preheated oven for 30–40 minutes (rolls will need 10–15 minutes). Turn the loaf out into a clean cloth and tap the underside; if it sounds hollow it is cooked. Allow the bread to cool on a cooling rack and dust with a little fresh flour.

english wholemeal bread

575 g wholemeal flour at room temperature
2 tsp salt
2 tsp easy-blend dried yeast
400 ml warm water

Butter a 900 g loaf tin and preheat the oven to 230ºC. Put the flour into a large bowl and add the salt and yeast. Mix together and make a well for the water. Add the water and mix with a wooden spoon to form a dough. Transfer the dough to the work surface and knead and stretch it. Place it in the buttered loaf tin, cover with a slightly damp tea towel and allow to rise in a warm part of the kitchen for 45 minutes to 1 hour.

When the dough is at the top of the loaf tin, bake in the oven for approximately 45 minutes. Check it is cooked by turning out into a clean cloth and tapping the underneath; it should sound hollow if it is ready. Allow the bread to cool on a cooling rack and when required you can crisp it up in a hot oven (approximately 200ºC) for 5 minutes and dust with fresh flour.

brioche

A popular bread from France, brioche is enriched with extra butter and eggs, making it a bit like a cake. It is traditionally eaten for breakfast or as an afternoon snack. It freezes well, so keep a loaf or two for emergencies!

500 g strong white flour
1 heaped tsp easy-blend dried yeast
1 heaped tbsp unrefined sugar
250 g unsalted butter
100 ml warm water
6 eggs, beaten
1 tsp salt

Preheat the oven to 180ºC and butter a 900 g loaf tin or 2 or more smaller, shaped loaf tins.

Sift the flour into a bowl and add the yeast and sugar. Cream the butter until soft and add to the flour with the water, most of the beaten eggs (save some for the glaze) and salt. Mix until it becomes a dough and then knead it until manageable and not too sticky.

Put the dough into a bowl, cover with clingfilm and rest for 45 minutes to 1 hour, until the dough has doubled in size. Turn it out and knead it slightly to knock it back and remove any air pockets. Divide the dough into the amount of loaves you plan to cook. Knead each amount for a minute and then remove a small amount for the traditional 'top hat' of the brioche – about ¼ is usually enough.

Mould the large portion of dough into a ball and place it in the tin, seam-side down. Make a hole in the top of the ball with a floured forefinger, mould the 'top hat' into a teardrop shape and push it, pointed-end down, into the hole. Press down to seal. Repeat with the other tins if using more than one, and place in a warm part of the kitchen to rise until the dough reaches the height of the tin.

Glaze with the remaining egg and bake for approximately 30 minutes, or until golden brown.

To make sure that it is cooked properly, unmould the loaf from its tin into a clean cloth and tap the underneath with your knuckles; if it sounds hollow it is cooked.

greek pitta bread

This famous Greek bread makes ideal pockets to serve with a selection of vegetable dishes and dips.

750 g strong white flour
2 tsp salt
1 tsp easy-blend dried yeast
400 ml warm water
1 tbsp olive oil

Sift the flour into a bowl and add the salt and the yeast. Now add the water, gradually moulding the mixture into a smooth dough (this is easier to do in a food processor).

Divide the dough into 12 equal lumps and knead each one. Shape into a ball and then flatten each ball with your hands into an oval shape. Drizzle a little olive oil onto a warm tray and lay out the dough ovals.

Allow to rise a little while you heat the grill to a medium-high heat. Sprinkle each pitta with a little cold water and grill quickly so that they puff up and brown – do not let them over-cook.

Flip over to brown the other side and serve immediately.

indian-style deep-fried brown bread

This is a great accompaniment to Asian dishes, and you must feel free to add crushed garlic or coriander seeds.

225 g wholemeal flour
½ tsp salt
2 tbsp light oil
90 ml warm water
vegetable oil for frying

Sift the flour and salt into a large bowl, add the oil and water and stir into a stiff dough. Transfer the dough to a floured surface and knead for a few minutes until smooth. Divide the mixture into 15–20 balls. Using a rolling pin, flatten the balls into oblong shapes 12 cm long on an oiled surface.

Heat the oil in a large pan or deep-fat fryer to 175ºC. Drop in the dough balls 4 at a time, stirring and pressing them down with a slotted spoon.

Cook until light brown and puffed up, approximately 4 minutes on each side. Drain and serve hot.

WEIGHTS AND MEASURES

The following charts give quick and easy reference for gauging oven temperatures and converting metric to imperial.

weights

15 g	½ oz
25 g	1 oz
50 g	1¾ oz
75 g	2¾ oz
100 g	3½ oz
125 g	4½ oz
450 g	1 lb
500 g	1 lb 2 oz
1 kg	2 lb 4 oz

volume

15 ml	½ fl oz
30 ml	1 fl oz
50 ml	2 fl oz
100 ml	3½ fl oz
250 ml	9 fl oz
500 ml	18 fl oz
600 ml	20 fl oz (1 pint)

oven temperatures

110ºC	225ºF	Gas mark ¼
130ºC	250ºF	Gas mark ½
140ºC	275ºF	Gas mark 1
150ºC	300ºF	Gas mark 2
170ºC	325ºF	Gas mark 3
180ºC	350ºF	Gas mark 4
190ºC	375ºF	Gas mark 5
200ºC	400ºF	Gas mark 6
220ºC	425ºF	Gas mark 7
230ºC	450ºF	Gas mark 8
240ºC	475ºF	Gas mark 9

index

RECIPE INDEX

acknowledgements

Carroll & Brown would also like to thank the following:
Salima Hirani; Laura Price; and everyone who lent us props,
including The Conran Shop and Sarah Lowman.

Photographic sources 8 (left and right) David Murray; 9 (top)
Tony Stone Images, (bottom) Telegraph Colour Library; 11 (left)
The Image Bank, (right) The Stock Market; 14 Telegraph Colour
Library; 15 Elizabeth Whiting Associates; 19 Elizabeth Whiting
Associates; 22 Telegraph Colour Library; 23 Telegraph Colour
Library; 24 Tony Stone Images; 26 The Image Bank; 83 (top and
bottom right) Carroll & Brown, (bottom left) Ocean Home Shop-
ping; 87 (top) Elizabeth Whiting Associates; 88 (left and right)
IKEA; 93 (bottom left) Telegraph Colour Library; 95 (bottom left)
Carroll & Brown; 104/5 Pictor International; 112/113 IKEA; 113
(top) Elgin & Hall; 119 (top) IKEA; 124 (bottom left) Telegraph
Colour Library; 127 (top left) Pictor International; 128 The Image
Bank; 130 (right) Telegraph Colour Library; 132 The Image Bank;
135 (right) Telegraph Colour Library; 137 The Image Bank; 140
Tony Stone Images; 141 Chris Gascoigne, VIEW; 144 Tony Stone
Images; 145 (middle) Telegraph Colour Library.

about the authors

SIMON BROWN qualified as a design engineer before he became
interested in Oriental medicine in 1981 and qualified as a Shiatsu
therapist and Macrobiotic consultant. During the same period, he
studied Feng Shui with Japanese masters in the USA. For seven
years, Simon was the director of London's Community Health Foundation, a centre offering a wide range of courses specialising in the
Oriental healing arts, giving it up in 1993 to make Feng Shui his
full-time career. Simon's clients include well-known celebrities,
such as Boy George, and large public companies, including The
Body Shop and British Airways.

Simon is author of the UK's best-selling *Practical Feng Shui*
(Cassell & CO), as well as *The Principles of Feng Shui* (Thorsons),
Feng Shui in a Weekend (Hamlyn), *Practical Feng Shui for Business*
(Ward Lock), *Essential Feng Shui* (Ward Lock), *Feng Shui Solutions*
(Cassell & CO), *Practical Astrology by Numbers* (Carroll & Brown) and
The Practical Art of Face Reading (Carroll & Brown). Simon has
written numerous articles for *Feng Shui For Modern Living*,
Cosmopolitan and *Vogue*, as well as a weekly column for the *Satur-
day Express*. He has also been involved in a number of radio and
television programmes.

Contact Simon at his website: www.chienergy.co.uk
or by telephone or fax on 0044 (0) 207 431 9897
or by e-mail on simon@chienergy.co.uk

STEVEN SAUNDERS, a Master Chef of Great Britain with out-
standing energy and creativity skills, was trained at London's Savoy
Hotel and set up his first restaurant, The Pink Geranium, in 1987
with his wife Sally. In 1991, Steven was awarded the title
Restaurateur of the Year in the UK, and in 1995 The Pink Geranium
was awarded the title Restaurant of the Year. In 1995, Steven was
involved in the hit cookery show Ready, Steady, Cook for the BBC.
The programme was awarded the title Cookery Show of the Year in
1998, making Steven Saunders into a cooking celebrity. Steven has
continued his television success with a number of cookery shows in
the UK and abroad. Steven acquired a second restaurant, Sheene
Mill, in Cambridge, in 1997 and it has since been named one of the
most fashionable restaurants outside of London.

1998 brought Steven his successful consultancy role at
'Steven Saunders at The Lowry' in Manchester. Steven also has his
own Organic Cookery School, a restaurant consultancy company
together with a prestigious outside catering company called
'Organica'. Steven's other books include: *Only the Best* (Little
Brown), *Chef's Secrets* (Boxtree), *Here's One I Made Earlier* (Channel
4 TV books), *Short Cuts* (Macmillan) and *Manchester on a Plate*
(Black & White).

Contact Steven at his website: www.stevensaunders.co.uk
or by telephone:
PR Vicky Daniels-Clark, Sheene Mill on 0044 (0) 1763 261393
or by e-mail on vicky@stevensaunders.co.uk